Fai
Leadership Lessons from the Lives of the Exiles

Regent College
MARKETPLACE INSTITUTE

The Regent College Marketplace Institute is a theological research and design institute at Regent College in Vancouver, Canada, committed to the communication of the gospel as public truth. The Institute develops resources, frameworks, and tools for integrating faith and public life, in order to support the transformation of individuals, communities, sectors, and the marketplace of ideas.

Faith and Politics: Leadership Lessons from the Lives of the Exiles

Preston Manning

Regent College Publishing
www.regentpublishing.com

Faith and Politics: Leadership Lessons from the Lives of the Exiles
Copyright © 2016 Preston Manning

All rights reserved. No part of this publication may be reproduced, stored in a retrieval system, or transmitted, in any form or by any means, electronic, mechanical, photocopying, recording or otherwise, without the prior written permission of the author, except in the case of brief quotations embodied in critical articles and reviews.

Published 2016 by Regent College Publishing
for the Regent College Marketplace Institute
http://marketplace.regent-college.edu

Regent College Publishing
5800 University Boulevard, Vancouver, BC V6T 2E4 Canada
Web: www.regentpublishing.com
E-mail: info@regentpublishing.com

Regent College Publishing is an imprint of the Regent Bookstore <www.regentbookstore.com>. Views expressed in works published by Regent College Publishing are those of the author and do not necessarily represent the official position of Regent College <www.regent-college.edu>.

ISBN 978-1-57383-529-9

Cataloguing in Publication information is on file at Library and Archives Canada.

Cover Image: *Daniel in the Lion's Den* by Peter Paul Rubens, 1615.

Except where noted, Scripture taken from the Holy Bible, NEW INTERNATIONAL VERSION®, NIV® Copyright © 1973, 1978, 1984, 2011 by Biblica, Inc.® Used by permission. All rights reserved worldwide.

NEW INTERNATIONAL VERSION® and NIV® are registered trademarks of Biblica, Inc. Use of either trademark for the offering of goods or services requires the prior written consent of Biblica US, Inc.

Contents

Preface vii
Introduction xi

1. The Sovereignty of God 1
2. Providential Positioning 16
3. Deliverance from Evil 34
4. The Counter-Transformation of Evil into Good 43
5. The Good and Evil of Bureaucracies 54
6. Safeguarding Public Bureaucracies from Doing Harm 67
7. Diligence and Excellence 83
8. Cooperation and Compromise 94
9. Re-establishing the Faith Community under Hostile Conditions 110

Preface

Regent College is a graduate school of Christian theology located in Vancouver, Canada, on the campus of the University of British Columbia. Our mission specifically includes assisting Christians to connect the gospel of Christ with every aspect of life—culture, science, media, business, and, yes, politics.

As citizens of the kingdom of God but also citizens of our country and the world, we are affected by domestic and international politics in a myriad of ways. Politics affect our freedoms and responsibilities, who governs us and how, the type of education our children receive, our incomes and employment opportunities, our taxes and what they are used for, the quality of our environment, our health and old age security, our collective response to the needs of the poor and oppressed, the safety of our streets, and whether we live in a time of war or a time of peace.

At Regent we believe that Jesus' call is for his followers to be salt and light in their communities and places of work,

Preface

to be ambassadors for him, to carry out the ministry of reconciliation, and to communicate the truth of the gospel to every nation. This is a call to relate the truth and person of Christ to every sphere of life, including the political.

One way of doing so is to study and act on lessons derived from the lives and experiences of God's servants in the past who have been called to involvement in the politics of their day. Such studies are particularly relevant when they are conducted through the eyes and interpreted through the experiences of contemporary Christians who have been involved in the politics of our day.

Hence, a series of booklets on leadership lessons from the lives of major Biblical figures authored by Preston Manning, a practicing Christian, a former Senior Fellow of Regent's Marketplace Institute, founder of two Canadian federal political parties, and former Leader of the Official Opposition in the Canadian House of Commons.

The first two booklets presented lessons in leadership from the lives of Moses[1] and David.[2] In this booklet, Mr. Manning presents lessons in leadership from the lives of Joseph, Daniel, Esther, Ezra, and Nehemiah—believers in the one true God but living in exile in Egypt, Babylon, and Medo-Persia, that is, in cultures and political systems indifferent or hostile to their faith.

Preface

There is, therefore, much for Christians today with political interests and ambitions to learn from "the lives of the exiles," especially as interpreted by a contemporary Christian with significant political experience. In the following pages, please join us as we study *Faith and Politics: Leadership Lessons from the Lives of the Exiles.*

Notes

1. Preston Manning, *Faith and Politics: Lessons in Leadership from the Life of Moses* (Vancouver: Regent College Publishing, 2013).

2. Preston Manning, *Faith and Politics: Lessons in Leadership from the Life of David* (Vancouver: Regent College Publishing, 2015).

Introduction

Moses and David were servants of God who exercised political leadership in a community—the nation of Israel—where their faith was generally shared by the people they were called to lead. But Joseph, Daniel and his friends, and Esther were servants of God who rose to positions of political leadership in societies and political systems that were hostile to their faith. Their circumstances were therefore more analogous to the situation of Christian believers today who attain positions of political leadership in the secular societies of our time—societies which, if they tolerate religious faith at all, relegate its expression to the private sphere and seek to purge its presence and influence from the public square. Lessons in leadership taught by the experiences of Joseph, Daniel, and Esther—serving from a minority position in a hostile majority culture and walking the difficult line between cooperation and compromise—are particularly relevant to believers who attain positions of political leadership in the materialistic, humanistic, and secular societies of today.

Introduction

Ezra and Nehemiah, while they were first and foremost leaders of God's people, had the unenviable task of trying to restore the life and vitality of a defeated and discouraged faith community immersed in a hostile environment. Their experience is also particularly relevant to spiritual leaders today who seek to carve out a spiritual homeland and rebuild spiritual institutions from a minority position under conditions hostile to faith.

According to the scriptural record, Joseph rose to a position of political influence in Egypt (in the 19th century BC) long before the revelation of God's purposes and laws to Moses and the organization of Israel into a political entity. Daniel on the other hand first achieved political influence in Babylon twelve or thirteen centuries later, with the nation of Israel now in captivity and in decline as a political entity. It is appropriate, nevertheless, to examine their lives together since Joseph and Daniel also had much in common.

Both were cruelly separated from their families at an early age, becoming exiles in foreign lands and cultures. Both were unjustly accused of crimes, imprisoned, and later vindicated. Both steadfastly adhered to their faith in God during these and other trying circumstances. Both rose to prominence through their God-given ability to interpret the troubling dreams and visions of ungodly rulers. Both came to be recognized as wise counsellors and competent

Introduction

managers of public affairs. And both eventually attained political positions second in power and influence only to the absolute monarchs they served.

I am of course aware that in scholarly circles the accuracy and historicity of the biblical stories of Joseph, Daniel, and the other "exiles" have been the subjects of much dispute. If a Hebrew slave named Joseph actually became Pharaoh's right-hand man in rescuing Egypt from a great famine, why is there not substantial corroborating evidence in the Egyptian historical records? Did a Jewish exile named Daniel actually live and serve politically in the Babylon of the sixth century BC, or is it not much more likely that the book of Daniel was written as a tract four centuries later to bolster the faith of the Jewish people during the intense persecutions of the Maccabean period?

I am not academically qualified to enter into such disputes nor do I care to do so. I accept the traditional view that such people actually lived and served as described in the canon of Scripture and as accepted by multitudes of Jewish and Christian scholars and believers over the centuries.[1] For me these stories have the ring of both spiritual and political authenticity, which makes them highly instructive for anyone who is personally active at the interface of faith and politics from a minority position.

So let us now look at *Leadership Lessons from the Lives*

Introduction

of the Exiles—Joseph, Daniel and his friends, Esther, Ezra, and Nehemiah—with the prayerful intent of applying those lessons toward participation as citizens and leaders in the political culture and systems of our times.

Notes

1. Joseph is believed to have lived during the 19th century BC. Daniel was among an early group of deportees to Babylon at the time of Nebuchadnezzar's first defeat of Jerusalem (around 603 BC) when he was a very young man. After Nebuchadnezzar, Daniel would serve his successor Belshazzar, Darius the Mede, and Cyrus the Persian. Cyrus the Great was the ruler who issued the decree authorizing Ezra to commence rebuilding the temple in 535 BC. Esther became Queen of the Medes and Persians around 473 BC in the reign of Xerxes I. Nehemiah commenced rebuilding the walls of Jerusalem around 445 BC.

Leadership Lessons from the Lives of the Exiles

1

The Sovereignty of God

Faith in the Sovereignty of God

Belief in the "sovereignty of God" is belief in God's supremacy—that all things are under his rule and control and that nothing happens without his direction or permission. It is belief in the God "who works out everything in conformity with the purpose of his will"[1] and who declared to the Israelites through the prophet Isaiah, "What I have said, that I will bring about; what I have planned, that I will do."[2]

For the ancient Hebrews it may have been relatively easy to believe in the sovereignty of God when they were living in their own land under the Law of God, triumphing in battle over their pagan enemies, worshiping God in their own temple, and living under the rule of kings whom they believed to be "the Lord's anointed." But this faith in God's supremacy was shaken to its foundations when Israel was conquered by the Assyrians and Judah by the Babylonians, when their rulers were executed or led away in chains, when the temple was desecrated and destroyed by a foreign army, and when the survivors of these disasters became exiles in foreign lands whose rulers and people were hostile or at best indifferent to the beliefs and practices of the people of God.

The question "How could God allow…?"—the question believers and sceptics alike invariably ask in times of trouble and calamity—gnawed away at the very foundations of their faith. How could one believe in the sovereignty and supremacy of God after these calamities? And even if one retained one's faith in God, how could one practise it in environments so indifferent or hostile to it?

Thus arose the sad lament of the believer in exile, "How can we sing the songs of the Lord while in a foreign land?"[3]

The Exile of the Modern Believer

Persecuted Christian minorities living in Muslim countries or under militantly atheistic regimes such as those in North Korea and China can readily identify with the situation of the Jewish exiles in Babylon. But so can contemporary Christian believers living in the materialistic, humanistic, and secular societies of the western world.

At one time the Christian faith occupied a respected and influential position in these societies. Today it is increasingly banished to the private sphere or at worst attacked and

The Sovereignty of God

declared irrelevant and antithetical to "progress" in education, science, law, the arts, the media, business, and politics.

In the political realm in Canada, it is now considered taboo to speak of your own most deeply held religious convictions, or those of your constituents, in the House of Commons or the provincial legislatures, notwithstanding the declarations of our Charter of Rights and Freedoms that "Everyone has the following fundamental freedoms: (a) freedom of conscience and religion; (b) freedom of thought, belief, opinion, and expression ...."[4]

Ironically, the preamble to that Charter actually begins with the phrase "Whereas Canada is founded upon principles that recognize the supremacy of God and the rule of law...." But when this phrase—the supremacy of God—has been appealed to as relevant to moral issues before the courts, it has been dismissed as "a dead letter" and irrelevant to the secular Canada of today.

In a 1999 child pornography case before the BC Court of Appeal, the judge dismissed moral arguments rooted in the Charter's recognition of the supremacy of God, with these words:

> "I accept that the law of this country is rooted in its religious heritage. But I know of no case on the *Charter* in which any court of this country has relied on the words Mr. Staley invokes [i.e., 'principles

that recognize the supremacy of God']. They have become a dead letter and while I might have wished the contrary, this Court has no authority to breathe life into them for the purpose of interpreting the various provisions of the *Charter*.... The words of the preamble relied upon by Mr. Staley can only be resurrected by the Supreme Court of Canada."[5]

Note that the judge not only dismisses arguments based on a Christian conception of morality, but does so in language as offensive as possible to Christians—pronouncing the supremacy of God to be a "dead letter" capable of "resurrection" only by the Supreme Court.

As for the Supreme Court of Canada, in a 1993 case dealing with physician-assisted suicide, Chief Justice Lamer declared Canada to be a "secular society" in which the court was not obliged to be guided in any way by "theological considerations."

"Can the right ... to choose suicide, be described as an advantage of which the appellant is being deprived? In my opinion, the Court should answer this question without reference to the philosophical and theological considerations fuelling the debate on the morality of suicide or euthanasia. It should consider the question before it from a legal perspective ... while keeping in mind that the Charter has established the essentially secular nature of Canadian society."[6]

And so as contemporary Christians, many of us find ourselves asking the same questions which perplexed the Jewish exiles in Babylon centuries ago. How could a sovereign God allow this to happen? How can one continue to believe in the supremacy of God in such circumstances? And from a practical standpoint, even if we retain our faith, how can and should we practise it in indifferent or hostile environments?

For answers to these questions, let us then look to the experience of the Jewish exiles and the initial leadership given to them by the prophet Jeremiah.

Jeremiah's Letter—Expanding the Exiles' Conception of the Sovereignty of God

Jeremiah as you may recall was the prophet who ministered from about 626 to 586 B.C. and witnessed the destruction of Jerusalem and the Temple in 587 BC. He prophesied the destruction of Judah as a nation and the exile of the Jewish people to Babylon as a result of their alienation from God by sin. But he also ministered to the exiles with messages of instruction concerning how they were to live in their new circumstances and messages of hope for the future.

> This is the text of the letter that the prophet Jeremiah sent from Jerusalem to … the people Nebuchadnezzar

had carried into exile from Jerusalem to Babylon. ... "This is what the Lord Almighty, the God of Israel, says to all those I carried into exile from Jerusalem to Babylon: 'Build houses and settle down; plant gardens and eat what they produce. Marry and have sons and daughters; find wives for your sons and give your daughters in marriage, so that they too may have sons and daughters. Increase in numbers there; do not decrease. Also, seek the peace and prosperity of the city to which I have carried you into exile. Pray to the Lord for it, because if it prospers, you too will prosper.' "[7]

Note the radical proposition that Jeremiah advances—that the Lord Almighty says that *he,* not Nebuchadnezzar, is the one who has carried them into exile from Jerusalem to Babylon. In the same letter he repeats this assertion twice: "Seek the peace and prosperity of the city to which *I (the God of Israel)* have carried you into exile. ... Therefore, hear the word of the Lord all you exiles whom *I* have sent away from Jerusalem to Babylon."[8]

Just as God's people were in his hand when they were in the Promised Land singing psalms by the river Jordan and under the authority of divinely anointed kings, so are they still in his hand while exiled to a foreign land, in mourning by the rivers of Babylon, and subject to foreign kings who are also ultimately under God's authority. In other words, the first prerequisite for God's people to survive and serve him in exile conditions is an expanded belief in the sovereignty of God.

Jeremiah's Letter—Instruction on How to Live Faithfully in Exile

The exiles are then given God's instructions through Jeremiah as to how they are to live faithfully in exile.

1. Settle Down and Build

Settle down, build houses and families, engage in productive work (agriculture, in this case) that you may increase in number and not decrease.

2. Pray

God is reachable by prayer from Babylon just as he was from Judea. Pray specifically for the peace and prosperity of the place where God has relocated you so that you may prosper from its prosperity.

3. Disregard False Spiritual Advice

You are to disregard the voices and visions of false and immoral prophets who counsel you to act contrary to these instructions.

This is apparently a reference to false prophets like Hananiah whose confrontation with Jeremiah is described in the chapter preceding Jeremiah's letter to the exiles.[9] Hananiah, like Jeremiah, prefaces his instructions to the exiles with "This is what the Lord Almighty, the God of Israel, says." But in effect he tells the exiles there is no need to settle down in or to pray for Babylon. Your exile there, he tells them, will be temporary because "within two years" God will "break the yoke of the king of Babylon" and bring you back to Judah. Hananiah's advice to the exiles is similar to that of self-proclaimed prophets today who instruct Christians *not* to involve themselves in the societies, environments, and places where God has placed them because the return of Christ is imminent. It is particularly significant that Jeremiah appears to be more concerned about the exiles' being led astray by false prophets from among their own religious community than he is about their being led astray by the influence of the Babylonians.

4. Trust the Promises

Lastly, God, through Jeremiah, seeks to restore the courage and morale of the exiles by challenging them to trust in his promise for their ultimate spiritual and political restoration.

This is what the Lord says:

"When seventy years are completed for Babylon, I will come to you and fulfill my gracious promise to bring you back to this place.

For I know the plans I have for you," declares the Lord, "plans to prosper you and not to harm you, plans to give you hope and a future."[10]

Lessons in Leadership

In subsequent chapters we will look at lessons in leadership *by* the exiles in the hostile spiritual and political environment in which they found themselves. But in Jeremiah's letter we have an example of leadership being provided *to* the exiles by the prophet. What then would be the equivalent leadership message *to* believers living in exile among the materialistic, humanistic, and secular societies of today?

If those in positions of spiritual leadership were to draft letters under the inspiration of the Holy Spirit to believers embedded by the sovereignty of God in the business, academic, media, science, trades, or political communities of today, what might those letters say?

Or if those in such leadership positions were to draft letters analogous to those of the Apostle Paul—written to the small first-century Christian communities embedded by the sovereignty of God in larger, hostile societies—what might be the focus and content of an Epistle to the Believers in the Academy, an Epistle to the Believers in the Business Community, an Epistle to the Believers in the Media, an Epistle to the Believers in the Science Community, or an

Epistle to the Believers in the Political Community of today?

An Epistle to Believers in the Political Community

In the vast literature of Christendom there are volumes of commentary and instruction relevant to believers embedded in all the various functional constituencies of today's world, including the political. But I must say that when I was in active politics I was never aware of receiving or reading an "Epistle to the Believers in the Political Community" as explicit and instructional as the letter sent by Jeremiah to the believing exiles embedded in Babylon.[11] In retrospect, if I had, it might have read something like the following:

> This is what the Lord Almighty says[12] to all those he has carried into a hostile political environment:
>
> Recognize and believe that you are where you are, not by your own efforts or design or by those of your adversaries, but by my grace and sovereignty.[13] Therefore, conduct yourself as one who lives politically in a country "founded on principles that recognize the supremacy of God" even if the politicians, media, judges, and citizenry of your country do not.
>
> Settle down there, build and plant.[14] Settle down in the constituencies, in the parties, in the interest groups, in the political offices, in the parliaments, legislatures,

The Sovereignty of God

and municipal councils of that country—wherever I have led you politically—and be a constructive influence there. Seek a "better country" while serving the country where I have placed you.[15]

Expand my influence there by wisdom and graciousness,[16] and by persuasive example, so that your numbers do not decrease but increase because others are attracted to you and your positions. Be salt and light.[17]

Seek the enlightenment and peace of the political community—serving where possible as truth tellers[18] and reconcilers of conflicting interests.[19]

Pray for the political community, for your opponents, and for all those in authority, that it may be well with you and the community at large.[20]

Pray that my kingdom may come and my will be done on earth as it is in heaven.[21]

Disregard the voices and visions of false prophets who counsel you to retreat into a private sphere, isolating yourself from the political community in a false holiness. And reject the counsel of the zealots who urge you to arbitrarily impose your beliefs on others.

This is not the way of Jesus who invites rather than compels acceptance of his person and his teachings. Be strong and courageous, trusting in my promise to some day make the kingdoms of this world my kingdoms.[22]

Be assured that I have plans to prosper you (as I define prosperity) and not to harm you, plans to give you hope and a future in the places where you are and to which I lead you.[23]

Application

One of the God-given tasks of some of the believers reading this article may well be to draft and communicate such leadership epistles, declaring the sovereignty of God in and over all those diverse places in this present world where God has planted his people.

And is it not the responsibility of those of us so planted to receive such instruction and act in light of the expanded conception of the sovereignty of God that such epistles proclaim?

Notes

1. Ephesians 1:11
2. Isaiah 46:11
3. Psalm 137:1-4, "By the rivers of Babylon we sat and wept when we remembered Zion. There on the poplars we hung our harps, for there our captors asked us for songs, our tormentors demanded songs of joy; they said, 'Sing us one of the songs of Zion!' How can we sing the songs of the Lord while in a foreign land?"
4. The Canadian Charter of Rights and Freedoms, Part I of The Constitution Act, 1982, Schedule B to the Canada Act 1982 (UK), 1982, c. 11.
5. R. V. Sharpe, 1999 BCCA 416, 175 D.L.R. (4th) 1 (CA), Call at para. 79-80.
6. Rodriguez v. British Columbia (Attorney General), [1993] 3 S.C.R. 519, 1993 CanLII 75 (SCC).
7. Jeremiah 29:1, 4-7
8. Jeremiah 29:7, 20
9. See Jeremiah 28
10. Jeremiah 29:10-11
11. From 1967 to 1987 I was peripherally and sporadically involved in provincial and federal politics in the province of Alberta. But from 1987 to 1993 I was fully involved in the creation of a new federal political party, the Reform Party of Canada. And from 1993 to 2002 I was the federal Member of Parliament for Calgary Southwest in the Canadian House of Commons.

Notes, *continued*

12. In making any such assertion, the writer of the epistle needs to be absolutely sure that the words written are God's words and not merely those of the writer, i.e., they must be scripturally based in every respect.

13. Daniel 4:25. As Daniel communicated to Nebuchadnezzar, "… the Most High is sovereign over the kingdoms of men and gives them to anyone he wishes."

14. Jeremiah 29:5-6

15. Membership in the Order of Canada, Canada's highest civilian order, is accorded to those who exemplify the order's Latin motto, *desiderantes meliorem patriam*, meaning "they desire a better country," a phrase taken from Hebrews 11:16 (KJV).

16. Matthew 10:16. This is the "Great Guideline" that Jesus gave to his earliest followers before sending them out to do "public work" in his name: be wise as serpents and gracious as doves.

17. Matthew 5:13-16. At the very outset of his teachings in the Sermon on the Mount, Jesus instructs his followers to be salt and light, performing good deeds before men (publicly) that will cause them to praise God.

18. Philippians 4:8-9; Ephesians 4:15. Not only are believers to "think about" whatever is true, but we are also to be "speaking the truth in love."

19. 2 Corinthians 5:17-21. At its highest level, politics, especially for those in government, is about the reconciliation of conflicting interests. In the Christian doctrine and teaching on the "ministry of reconciliation" through the exercise of self-sacrificial love, we have Christ's example of how to reconcile conflicting interests at the deepest level.

Notes, *continued*

20. 1 Timothy 2:1-3, "I urge, then, first of all, that requests, prayers, intercession and thanksgiving be made for everyone—for kings and all those in authority, that we may live peaceful and quiet lives in all godliness and holiness. This is good, and pleases God our Savior…."

21. As Jesus taught us to pray in the "Lord's Prayer," Matthew 6:10.

22. Revelation 11:15

23. Jeremiah 29:11, the great promise given by Jeremiah to the believing exiles in Babylon.

2

Providential Positioning

"And who knows but you have come to your royal position for such a time as this?"

– Mordecai to Queen Esther when the Jews in Medo-Persia were threatened with genocide[1]

"Your Majesty... acknowledge that the Most High is sovereign over the kingdoms of men and gives them to anyone he wishes."

– Daniel to King Nebuchadnezzar of Babylon in interpreting the king's dream[2]

Introduction

In an earlier study entitled *Faith and Politics in the Life of Moses* we examined the concept of "providential positioning"—how Moses was uniquely positioned by God to play a leadership role in liberating Israel from Egypt by virtue of his princely position in Pharaoh's household while still being in contact, through his mother, with his Hebrew heritage.[3]

In a later study entitled *Faith and Politics: Lessons in Leadership from the Life of David* we saw a very different aspect of providential positioning and leading. In David's case there was very little in terms of family position or visible circumstances that would lead anyone—even the spiritually perceptive Samuel—to believe that the shepherd boy David could become a future King of Israel.[4]

Like Samuel, in seeking to ascertain whom God may have in mind for political and spiritual leadership, we need to be reminded that he "does not look on the things that man looks at. Man looks at the outward appearance, but the Lord looks at the heart."[5] And what the Lord sees and does there—especially if he perceives a yielded and contrite heart—can lead a shepherd (David) to the throne of Israel, a slave (Joseph) to become vice-ruler of Egypt, an orphan girl (Esther) to become Queen of the Medes and Persians, and a teenage exile (Daniel) to eventually become the First Minister of Babylon.

"For Such a Time as This"

All three of these believers—Joseph, Esther, and Daniel—attained high office and political influence in the non-believing societies in which they found themselves. It is significant, however, that it was major disasters and calamities, not far-sighted planning and ambitious ladder-climbing, that led them to their positions of influence.

In the case of Joseph, an impending famine and his God-given ability to interpret Pharaoh's predictive dream concerning it led Joseph to his political position. And his God-given wisdom in managing the response to that national calamity—storing up grain in advance of the famine and utilizing its distribution to secure ownership of the land for Pharaoh—maintained him in his position and increased his influence even more.

In the case of Daniel, it was again a God-given ability to interpret the obscure but predictive dream of the king of Babylon that gained him his position of political influence. He was then able to use that influence to save Babylon, at least in part, from the wild excesses to which Nebuchadnezzar was inclined, including the wholesale execution of his advisors, few if any of whom would have shared Daniel's faith.

And in the case of Esther, the "such a time as this" for which she was providentially positioned in Medo-Persia was a time when the exiled Jewish people were threatened with genocide—a threat which Esther's positioning and influence with King Xerxes enabled her to avert.

A 20th Century Example

So does God still work in this way—using disasters and calamities often brought on by mankind's fallen nature and propensity for greed and violence—to lead believers toward positions of public service and political influence?

Providential Positioning

I believe he does. In fact, one could argue that this is one of the chief mechanisms of "providentially positioning" believers in this world. "Who knows but that *you* are being led to political involvement and public service for such a time as this?"—the "such a time as this" being one of the contemporary economic, social, or political crises of our times, affecting many people, very few of whom may share your personal faith convictions.

For example, in Western Canada—one of two regions in our country (the other being Quebec) which tend to innovate politically by creating new political movements and parties—it was the Great Depression of the 1930s which led a number of professing Christians into positions of political prominence.

J. S. Woodsworth was a Methodist minister and proponent of the social gospel[6] who publicly sided with rioting workers during the great Winnipeg General Strike of 1919.[7] Together with Tommy Douglas, a Baptist minister, and others, he eventually formed a social democratic political party, the Cooperative Commonwealth Federation (CCF) which later became the present day New Democratic Party (NDP). The CCF/NDP were strong advocates of social justice, campaigning strenuously for old age pensions, unemployment insurance, and universal medical insurance coverage.

Another but similar example involves the other major western Canadian political party spawned by the Depression, namely the Social Credit Movement in Alberta. It was led by a Calgary high school principal and Christian layman, William Aberhart. Aberhart pioneered Christian radio broadcasting on the Canadian prairies in the 1920s, focusing on the personal salvation aspects of the gospel and his interpretation of the prophetic scriptures.[8]

Aberhart founded a training institute in Calgary, Alberta, for would-be ministers of which my father, Ernest C. Manning, was the first student. During the Depression that institute operated a soup kitchen to serve the poor and unemployed. In the long line-ups which formed outside it, Aberhart began to see former public-school students of his whom he had sent off to be teachers, doctors, and lawyers. But now they were "riding the rails" by the thousands, from city to city, searching in vain for work. The experience impelled Aberhart to search for answers to the Depression and he settled on the idea of social credit—a primitive form of Keynesian economics that maintained that the economic pump should be primed by expanding the money supply during times of economic contraction. Eventually Social Credit became a provincial political party, strongly supported by evangelicals, and formed the provincial government in Alberta in 1935 with Aberhart as Premier. My father succeeded Aberhart in 1943 and served for another 25 years as

Premier, all the time carrying on the evangelical radio ministry which Aberhart had pioneered in the 1920s.[9]

Whether or not one agrees with the political positions of Woodsworth and Douglas, Aberhart and Manning, or their respective interpretations of the Scriptures, there is no question but that it was their faith-based responses to an economic and social disaster, the Great Depression, which prompted their political actions and propelled them into positions of political influence.

What About You and the Leading of Contemporary Crises?

If God still works in this way—using disasters and calamities which are often the product of mankind's fallen nature—to lead believers toward positions of public service and political influence, what about you?

Could it be that *you* are being led by your Christian convictions to some such involvement by one of the many economic, social, and political crises that afflict our current world, regardless of whether the people of your community, province, or country share your personal faith convictions?

The Challenge of Caring for the Sick

Our world is periodically wracked by health crises—the AIDS disaster that began in Africa and is now worldwide;

the recent Ebola outbreak on that same continent; the SARS outbreak of 2003, which provided Canada with a foretaste of what a pandemic-like health crisis might be like and how to deal with it; and the increases in cancer cases, hereditary diseases, and end-of-life health issues that lead so many today to despair of life despite all the advances of modern medicine. Such crises challenge individuals, communities, governments, and societies to conduct medical research, to engage in health-care education, to pursue preventative and supportive private initiatives and public health-care policies, and of course to engage directly in the administration and delivery of medical care for the ill.[10]

Could it be that, for some Christian believers, a personal and acute consciousness of and concern for these health-care challenges constitutes "providential leading"—a providential call to become personally and actively involved in meeting the health-care needs of others in the Spirit of Christ? The New Testament abounds with stories of Jesus and his disciples being confronted with the needs of the sick and being directed by the Spirit to respond to them with compassion and care. The history of the western world includes numerous accounts of Christian believers who were confronted with health-care crises and out of their faith convictions risked their own health in order to respond to the needs of others. Could it be that a condition of our "times" of which you are acutely conscious is a health-care crisis that you are being led to address in some way? And could it be that God is putting to you the same question he posed to Esther long ago through Mordecai, "Who knows but you have come to your position"—a position of awareness of a need and the opportunity to help—"for such a time as this?"

The Challenge of Environmental Stewardship

Our world, including your local community, is increasingly faced with serious environmental challenges—the increasing degradation of soil, water, vegetation, and atmospheric conditions as a result of our insatiable appetite for goods and services and the means we employ to satisfy that appetite.

Could it be that for you as a Christian believer an increasing consciousness of and concern for environmental degradation constitutes "providential leading"—a providential call for you as a believer to act: to constrain your own demands for goods and services in the spirit of Christian self-sacrifice; to rediscover environmental stewardship and "creation care" as a spiritual obligation to our Creator and His creation; and to participate in issue and electoral campaigns to raise environmental conservation and responsible resource stewardship on the agendas of local, provincial, and national governments?

In other words, could it be that a condition of our "times" of which you are acutely conscious is environmental degradation—a condition that you are in a position to address in some way? Who knows but that you have come to that position for such a time as this?

The Challenge of Conflict Resolution

It is also true that our modern world abounds in conflicts—economic, social, environmental, cultural, and political. But could it be that the existence of conflict in whatever circumstances you find yourself again constitutes "providential positioning"—a providential call for you to exercise at a human level what the Apostle Paul called the ministry of reconciliation, serving as a self-sacrificial mediator of conflicting interests after the example of Jesus?[11]

In many respects, democratic politics at its most profound level is all about the reconciliation of conflicting interests by non-violent means. During my time in Canada's national politics one of the greatest and most worrisome conflicts facing the country was on the national unity front, with a growing portion of the political class and population of the province of Quebec desiring to secede from the Canadian federation.

My own awareness of this challenge—secession challenges being among the most dangerous crises that can afflict an established state—began in the 1960s and led me to study secession crises in other times and countries, especially federations,[12] and the various ways of dealing with them.[13] By the 1980s, growing discontents in western Canada were leading to the creation of an embryonic secessionist movement in the West as well, which, had it succeeded in gaining momentum, would have put intolerable strains on the federation and the national government, no matter who formed it. It was to address the underlying factors that were fuelling the western separatist movement—fiscal and economic mismanagement by the federal government and institutional indifference and unresponsiveness to legitimate western interests—that my colleagues and I formed the Reform Party of Canada with the slogan "The West Wants In."[14]

Our general approach was to give strong but responsible voice to western discontents while proposing reforms to the federation as a constructive alternative to tearing it apart. We subsequently elected a significant number of Members of Parliament and were active in the House of Commons and on the national unity front when the Quebec secession crisis was brought to a head in 1995 by a province-wide referendum on whether that province should secede or not. The referendum was won by the No side (No to secession) by the narrowest of margins[15] and legislation,[16] originally proposed by one of our members, was put in place to better equip the federal government to deal with secession crises of this type should they ever arise again.

During all this time I must confess that as a Christian believer participating in the politics of my country I was not particularly conscious that I and my Christian colleagues in Parliament might have come to our positions of influence, however modest that influence may have been, by providential leading for "such a time as this." During this period we received many briefs and representations from all sorts of interest groups on how best to deal or not deal with the unity crisis. But I cannot recall receiving any from the faith community or Christian organizations that raised this possibility or sought to specifically apply the Christian teaching on reconciliation to Canada's unity crisis in any practical way. In retrospect, however, Mordecai's question is surely relevant to our case—"Who can tell but that we were brought to our particular political positions for such a time as this?"

Christian believers who find themselves in positions of influence in such conflict situations in the future should be more acutely conscious of the possibility and direction of such "providential positioning"—positioning for the express purpose of playing a reconciling role.[17]

From Macro to Micro

Finally, it is important to recognize that the "crises" that may eventually lead to political involvement and influence

Providential Positioning

need not always be macro crises as described earlier. They may be micro crises—crises in the lives of individuals whom we encounter every day—the crises of individual and personal deprivation, poverty, sickness, abuse, alienation, loneliness, persecution, and bad choices.

Moses' first step toward his political role as the liberator of Israel from slavery in Egypt began with a personal incident in which he saw an Egyptian abusing a single Hebrew slave and felt compelled to intervene.

Toward the end of his earthly ministry Jesus spoke of the providential positioning of believers in the kingdom-that-is-to-come and linked that positioning to how we as his professed followers respond when confronted with these micro crises in the lives of others.

> "When the Son of Man comes in his glory. ... All the nations will be gathered before him, and he will separate the people one from another as a shepherd separates the sheep from the goats. He will put the sheep on his right and the goats on his left. Then the King will say to those on his right, 'Come, you who are blessed by my Father; take your inheritance, the kingdom prepared for you since the creation of the world. For I was hungry and you gave me something to eat, I was thirsty and you gave me something to drink, I was a stranger and you invited me in, I needed clothes and you clothed me, I was sick and you looked after me, I was in prison and you came to visit

me.' Then the righteous will answer him, 'Lord, when did we see you hungry and feed you, or thirsty and give you something to drink? When did we see you a stranger and invite you in, or needing clothes and clothe you? When did we see you sick or in prison and go to visit you?' The King will reply, 'Truly I tell you, whatever you did for one of the least of these brothers and sisters of mine, you did for me.' "[18]

Jesus was speaking of our personal responses to these personal crises in the lives of individuals we encounter. But if laws, public policy, public expenditures, and other actions of governments can have anything to do with alleviating the causes or effects of deprivation, poverty, sickness, alienation, loneliness, persecution, and bad choices it may well be that God will also use such encounters to lead some of us toward playing a political role in shaping collective responses to such micro crises just as he did with Moses and has done with others of his politically involved followers down through the ages.

In one sense engaging in economic, social, and political crises—whether on the macro or micro scale—is counter-intuitive. Our natural instinct is to avoid, even to flee, situations characterized by conflict, hatred, injury, uncertainty, despair, darkness, and sadness. But could it be, as it was in the case of believers in exile in times past, that it is these very conditions that constitute our providential calling

Providential Positioning

to involvement? And rather than avoiding them, we are to engage with them, praying the prayer known as the Prayer of St Francis of Assisi:

> Lord, make me an instrument of your peace,
> Where there is hatred, let me sow love;
> where there is injury, pardon;
> where there is doubt, faith;
> where there is despair, hope;
> where there is darkness, light;
> where there is sadness, joy.

As a believer in the providence of God but living in "exile" in a hostile world, whatever your position in time and relation to the crises and tragedies of our age both small and great, "Who can tell but that you have been brought to that position for such a time as this?"

Notes

1. Esther 4:14
2. Daniel 4:24-25
3. Preston Manning, *Faith and Politics in the Life of Moses* (Vancouver: Regent College Publishing, 2013).
4. Preston Manning, *Faith and Politics: Lessons in Leadership from the Life of David* (Vancouver: Regent College Publishing, 2014).
5. 1 Samuel 16:7
6. Woodsworth left the Methodist church over its emphasis on individual salvation while neglecting, in his judgment, the deplorable social and economic circumstances in which so many of those individuals lived. It was said that if you dropped Woodsworth's Bible on the floor it would open by virtue of frequent reference to the 10th chapter of Luke's gospel, the story of the Good Samaritan—a man who "loved his neighbor as himself," even someone of another race and religion—to whom Jesus pointed his hearers, saying, "Go and do likewise."
7. During the strike, which became quite violent, Woodsworth was charged with seditious libel for a speech he wrote and published using verses from the book of Isaiah as a text. The indictment read in part: "That J. S. Woodsworth ... unlawfully and seditiously published seditious libels in the words and figures following: 'Woe unto them that decree unrighteous decrees, and that write grievousness which they have prescribed; to turn aside the needy from judgment, and to take away the right from the poor of my people, that widows may be their prey and that they may rob the fatherless,' ISAIAH [10: 1-2]. 'And they shall build houses and inhabit them; and they shall plant vineyards, and eat the fruit of them. They shall not build and

Notes, *continued*

another inhabit; they shall not plant and another eat; for as the days of a tree are the days of my people, and mine elect shall long enjoy the work of their hands.' ISAIAH [65: 21-22]." The King vs. J. S. Woodsworth; Court of King's Bench for Manitoba, proceedings held in the City of Winnipeg, commencing November 4, 1919.

8. It was said that if you dropped Aberhart's Bible on the floor it would open by virtue of frequent reference to the 3rd chapter of John's gospel and Jesus' admonition to Nicodemus that he could not enter or serve the kingdom of God unless he was "born again" of God's spirit from within. Later commentators on these two religious streams that crossed the Canadian prairies in the 1920s and 30s have pointed out that if you put the vertical shaft of personal salvation and the horizontal crossbar of the social gospel together, you have the cross—the great symbol of the Christian faith and a more inclusive picture of the life and teachings of Jesus.

9. For a more thorough description of this period and the activities of William Aberhart and Ernest C. Manning see Brian Brennan, *The Good Steward: The Ernest C. Manning Story* (Fifth House Ltd., 2008).

10. Historians documenting the rise of Christianity in the Roman Empire have noted that it was the active and compassionate response of Christian believers toward the victims of the plagues (likely smallpox) which wracked the Empire in the 2nd and 3rd centuries—in contrast to the response of pagan leaders and physicians who tended to flee the scene—that increased the appeal of the Christian faith among the general population. To quote Charles Moore in Pandemic Love: "During the plague of Alexandria when nearly everyone else fled, the early Christians risked their lives for one another by simple deeds of washing the

Notes, *continued*

sick, offering food and water, and consoling the dying …. (They) not only took care of their own, but also reached far beyond themselves. … In an era when serving others was thought to be demeaning, the 'followers of the way,' instead of fleeing disease and death, went about ministering to the sick and helping the poor, the widowed, the crippled, the blind, the orphaned, and the aged. The people of the Roman Empire were forced to admire their works and dedication. 'Look how they love one another' was heard on the streets." Charles Moore, *Plough Weekly*, posted May 15, 2009, http://www.plough.com/en/articles/2009/pandemic-love (accessed August 19, 2015).

11. 2 Corinthians 5:17-21

12. In particular, I focused on studying the most prominent and disastrous secession crisis to afflict a major federation in the 19th century, namely the secession of the southern states from the American Union, which triggered the American Civil War. My focus was not on the war itself but on the thirty-year period preceding it and the various legislative, judicial, and political means employed in attempts to resolve the conflict between North and South by peaceful means.

13. See 1 Kings 11-14 and 2 Chronicles 10-12. It should be noted that the Old Testament itself contains a detailed and instructive account of a secession crisis, namely the secession of the northern tribes of Israel from the united kingdom established by Saul, David, and Solomon. This crisis, precipitated in part by the heavy taxes imposed by Solomon to finance the building of the temple and his palaces, and the ill-advised reaction of his son Rehoboam to Israel's demands for relief, had dire consequences for both Israel and Judah—civil war, religious apostasy, and eventually

Notes, *continued*

military defeat of the divided kingdom by the Assyrians and the Babylonians.

14. See Preston Manning, *Think Big: My Adventures in Life and Democracy* (McClelland & Stewart, 2002).

15. 1995 referendum results: No 50.6%, Yes 49.4%. Margin of victory, 1.2%.

16. Bill C-20, commonly called the "Clarity Act," passed into law in 2000. See S.C. 2000, c.26.

17. Some uncertainty as to whether we as believers have been "providentially positioned" to play a role in such situations is probably a good thing, guarding us against arrogant presumption and driving us to prayer, consultation of the Scriptures, and seeking the advice of fellow believers as to the course we should take. It is significant that Mordecai's counsel to Esther on this subject was given, not in the form of a declaration as to her duty in the situation in which she found herself, but in the form of a question: "Who knows but you have come to royal position for such a time as this?" Who knows? Presumably God knows, but it is up to Esther to decide whether and how to respond. And if she does not, Mordecai is convinced that God will still achieve his purposes. "For if you remain silent at this time, relief and deliverance will arise from another place, but you and your father's family will perish" (Esther 4:14).

18. Matthew 25:31-40

3

Deliverance from Evil

… Lead us not into temptation, but deliver us from the evil one.
– Jesus to his disciples in teaching them how to pray[1]

Do not be overcome by evil, but overcome evil with good.
– the Apostle Paul to the Christians in Rome[2]

While the contest with evil is a feature of the Christian experience no matter what our environment, its institutionalization and dominance is more likely to occur in societies that deny its existence and spiritual roots. It is therefore particularly important that believers living in exile in environments and societies hostile to faith and the things of God have a thorough understanding of the nature of evil, how it "works," and God's provisions for deliverance from its tactics and stratagems.

The Transformation of Good into Evil

I once read a commentary on the nature of good and evil by a German pastor who had survived the horrors of the

Second World War.[3] It is deeply relevant to any Christian believer but especially to those involved in and active at the interface of faith and politics.

He was reflecting painfully on the evil of the Nazi regime—its capacity to amplify and give licence to mankind's tendency toward prejudice, hatred, cruelty, brutality, and violence. But in retrospect what horrified him even more was its capacity to take that which was good and admirable in human beings—the industriousness of the German people and the idealism of German youth, for example—and twist even those elements to diabolical purposes.

The twisting of that which is good into something evil and destructive of human life is a major theme of both the Old and New Testaments. For example:

- In the Old Testament story of the Fall that which was pronounced by God himself to be "good" becomes cursed when the first human beings succumb to the temptations of the Evil One.[4]

- In the New Testament record of the trial of Jesus, the law of God, given as an instrument of righteousness and justice, is cited by Jesus' accusers in support of their demand that he, the Son of God, be crucified.[5]

If as Christians we find ourselves in the presence of such a transformation—evil fastening itself to something good and twisting it to destructive ends—it is no exaggeration to say that we are in the very presence of the devil (evil in its most virulent form) and need to be not only on guard but also in the forefront of resistance.

From Good to Evil in the Life of Joseph and of Israel

Joseph, for example, was a son much loved by his father Jacob—a good thing. But this good thing was somehow seized upon by the forces of evil and twisted, only slightly at first, into favouritism, which in turn begat jealousy and resentment among his brothers. Joseph at an early age also had a gift for prophetic dreaming—a good thing, a God-given gift which would later commend him to the pharaoh of Egypt. But while he was an adolescent the forces of evil were able to take two of his prophetic dreams that predicted that he would some day rule over his family and induce young Joseph to share them unwisely and arrogantly, further feeding the smoldering fire of jealousy and resentment among his brothers. Eventually that fire blazed into hatred, attempted murder, and the sale of Joseph into slavery. Evil affixed itself to that which was initially good in the life of Joseph and twisted it to evil and destructive ends—his life as a slave in exile in Egypt.

Israel and Judah were once part of a united kingdom, worshippers of the one true God and heirs to his promises. They were ruled by David, a man of God, whose two greatest desires toward the end of his reign were to be succeeded by a God-honouring son (Solomon) and to build a great dwelling place (the Temple) for God. These were good things—noble, spiritual, and conducive to life and happiness. But once again the forces of evil insinuated themselves, subtly at first, but shrewdly and tenaciously, into the religion and politics of the kingdom.

The desire and willingness of human beings, and the Israelites in particular, to "worship" made them vulnerable to the attraction of the gods of those around them. Not only did the people succumb to this attraction, but Solomon himself was eventually led astray to worship the gods of his many wives. In addition, Solomon's desire to bring glory to God by building a magnificent temple soon morphed into a desire to build magnificent palaces for the Lord's anointed—Solomon himself. The location of the Temple and Solomon's palaces in Jerusalem, in Judea, and the onerous taxes levied on the whole kingdom to pay for them, led to charges of favouritism and resentment among the northern tribes. This in turn blazed into open rebellion and civil war during the reign of Solomon's son Rehoboam. It also led to religious apostasy as the leaders of the northern tribes sought to provide an alternative place and form of worship to that provided by the temple and priests in Jerusalem. As a result God's people became divided and weakened spiritually, politically, and militarily—easy prey to the Assyrians and Babylonians who eventually conquered both Israel and Judah and led their people into exile and slavery. Evil insinuated itself into that which was initially good, and redirected it to evil and destructive ends.

Good to Evil in Our Day

In our own day, examples of this phenomenon also abound. The search for truth, meaning in life, and harmonious relationships through the search for God—genuine "religion" in its broadest sense—ought to be a boon and a blessing to mankind in the here-and-now as well as in the world to come. In Canada, for example, many of the foundation stones of our health, educational, and social welfare services were laid by people whose faith led them to self-sacrificial service to others. And it was faith in God that enabled many of my parents' generation to endure the hardships and terrors of the Great Depression and the Second World War.

But far too often the search for meaning and meaningful service in life through faith has been perverted and twisted to become a force for evil—a source of tyranny, persecution, religious wars, and the present-day jihads of religious extremists. It has gone from good to evil on the religious front, something terribly discouraging to the sincere believer and driving millions away from God rather than toward him.

In the political world, the pursuit of freedom down

through the ages has brought the blessings of religious, intellectual, political, and economic liberty to millions in what are now regarded as free societies. But it is also true that freedom, especially freedom exercised without responsibility, can be carried to extremes so that liberation movements—from the Renaissance, the Reformation, and the French Revolution to the sexual liberation movement of the twentieth century—can also be transformed into new tyrannies and new sources of suffering.

Science and technology, benevolently developed and used, have been enormous forces for good, increasing the life span and improving the health and wellbeing of billions of human beings. But it is also a sad reality that virtually every major scientific and technological advancement—from the discovery and harnessing of fire and gunpowder, to nuclear fission and fusion, to the discovery and manipulation of the genomes of living organisms—can also be harnessed to the science of warfare and the destruction of human life.

With respect to the provision of health care, education, and social services—efforts vital to the wellbeing of millions of people—bureaucracy is the predominant organizational structure adopted for their management and delivery. But that very same organizational form can also become an instrument for harm—stifling freedom and initiative, reducing human beings to mere names or numbers in a file, and dividing responsibility among so many levels and agents that no one accepts responsibility or can be held accountable for the effectiveness or morality of outcomes.

It is as if great good, through faith, freedom, science, and bureaucracy, and great evil, through the abuse and perversion of the same, are opposite sides of a very thin coin often balancing precariously on its edge. And, depending on the intentions and strength of those in positions of influence at a particular point in time, just a small nudge is all that is required for that coin to fall good-side-up or evil-side-up with great blessing or great tragedy as the inevitable result.

Personal Application

So what about us? If there truly is such a diabolic thing as good being twisted into evil, is it not important for us to identify and examine the instances in our own lives and work where the forces of evil may have fastened onto things which are inherently good and twisted them into something bad? Perhaps it is our conviction of sin turned into depression and paralyzing feelings of worthlessness; our passion for the things of Christ morphing into intemperate zeal that repels rather than attracts others; our desire to succeed and set a good example twisted into self-promotion and workaholic behaviours; or our desire to do and see others "do things right" pushed into obsessive perfectionism and criticism of others.

The challenge is to be alert to the possibilities and realities of good being twisted into evil so that we seek God's help in guarding against and resisting such transformations. We truly need to pray frequently and earnestly as Jesus taught us, "Lead us not into temptation, but deliver us from the evil one."[6] The good news, to be explored in the next chapter, is that it is at these very points of spiritual vulnerability—in ourselves, our work, or the institutions of which we are a part—that God's grace can begin its work of prevention and counter-transformation.

Notes

1. Matthew 6:13
2. Romans 12:21
3. I read this commentary many years ago, and cannot today recall its source. It would be appreciated if any reader who can identify the source and author would advise me so that proper reference can be made and credit given.
4. Genesis 1-3
5. John 19:7
6. Matthew 6:13

4

The Counter-Transformation of Evil Into Good

You intended to harm me (by selling me into slavery in Egypt), but God intended it for good to accomplish what is now being done, the saving of many lives.

– Joseph to his brothers[1]

The good news of the Christian gospel writ large is that there is a counter-balance for "good into evil." In the providence of God "where sin increased, grace (the unmerited favour of God) increased all the more."[2] Evil can be overcome with good, even transformed into good, and God's servants have an integral part to play in working with him to bring about such counter-transformations.

The most striking example of this phenomenon in the Christian narrative is the transformation of the cross—a cruel instrument of torture and death—into an instrument for achieving the forgiveness of sins and the salvation of mankind through Christ's sacrificial death upon it.

When we find ourselves in the presence of such a counter-transformation we are in the very presence of God—goodness personified and in its purest form.

Evil to Good in the Life of Joseph

Joseph, as we have already seen, experienced the good life of a privileged son in a God-blessed family transformed by the evil actions of his brothers into the life of a lowly slave in a foreign land.

But the greatest and most inspirational aspect of Joseph's life is that he also experienced the counter-transformation—evil transformed into good—with that transformation being the dominant and lasting influence in his life.

As a slave in the household of Potiphar, he rises by virtue of his ability and diligence to be put in charge of the entire household. When he is unjustly accused of attacking Potiphar's wife, he suffers yet another crushing reversal as he is cast into prison. In the prison, again by virtue of his administrative ability and trustworthiness, he is put in charge of other prisoners. There he meets two servants of Pharaoh, his cupbearer and baker, who have been imprisoned for their faults. Joseph correctly interprets their dreams and the cupbearer is restored to his position

Counter-Transformation of Evil Into Good

in Pharaoh's household. But the cupbearer forgets Joseph who continues to languish in prison until Pharaoh is also troubled by a dream which none of his advisors can interpret. The cupbearer then remembers Joseph who is summoned from prison to interpret Pharaoh's dream of an impending famine. When Joseph does so and proposes the policy that will safeguard Egypt from that disaster, he is promoted to the position of vice-ruler of Egypt. When his brothers come to Egypt to buy food, he reveals himself to them, rescues his entire family from starvation, resettles them in Egypt, and gives this remarkable testimony to the work of God in transforming evil into good:

> Then Joseph said to his brothers, "Come close to me." When they had done so, he said, "I am your brother Joseph, the one you sold into Egypt! And now, do not be distressed and do not be angry with yourselves for selling me here, because it was to save lives that God sent me ahead of you ... to preserve for you a remnant on earth and to save your lives by a great deliverance. So then, it was not you who sent me here, but God. ... You intended to harm me, but God intended it for good to accomplish what is now being done, the saving of many lives."[3]

In Joseph's life, his abilities and ambition for leadership and his gifts for prophetic dreaming and interpretation were initially seized upon by evil forces and used against him with tragic and destructive results. But then came the more powerful and lasting counter-transformation; God in his mercy and providence took those same abilities, ambitions, and gifts, and redirected their manifestation and use for good, "the saving of many lives."

The Role of Believers in Effecting Counter-Transformations

It seems to me, therefore, that three of the primary roles of believers occupying positions of influence in the nonbelieving, secular, and materialistic societies and systems of today are:

- To be aware of the distinct possibility that the good with which we may be associated may be transformed into evil in our lives and areas of influence.

- To be alert to God's call to be on guard against and resistant to such transformations, and cooperate with him in resisting them.

- To be alert to God's working to effect counter-transformations—good from evil—and to join with him in such work.

Certainly those of us who live as believing exiles in societies indifferent or hostile to our faith—as Joseph, Daniel, and Esther did—have ample opportunity to exercise these three roles.

My illustrations of those opportunities and possible responses are primarily drawn from my experiences as a management consultant and an elected politician living and working in the largely secular society that Canada has become. But hopefully the sharing of them will suggest similar opportunities and responses to you no matter what your position or field of work.

Preventing and Combatting the Abuse of Freedom

In Canada, the *Charter of Rights and Freedoms* affirms: "Everyone has the following fundamental freedoms: (a) freedom of conscience and religion; (b) freedom of thought, belief, opinion, and expression, including freedom of the press and other media of communications; (c) freedom of peaceful assembly; and (d) freedom of association."[4]

I personally believe that Christians should be in the forefront of championing freedom, in particular the freedom of conscience and belief on which religious and political freedom depends. I am also of the view that freedom is indivisible; a threat to one freedom, such as freedom of conscience, is a threat to all freedoms, and therefore to be resisted.

But as Christian believers acutely conscious of mankind's fallen nature and propensity for evil, do we not also have a special role to play in recognizing the potential in ourselves and others for abusing freedom—exercising freedom irresponsibly and toward destructive ends—and the need to prevent and combat such abuses?

For example, I am a believer in the freedom of economic enterprise and when I was in the management consulting business I had ample opportunity to assist clients in the energy sector in the exercise of that freedom. But, as a Christian believer I was also acutely conscious of the potential for individuals and corporations to abuse freedom of enterprise and the opportunities afforded by free markets. Gradually, I found my consulting practice led, by this awareness rather than by design, into assisting energy companies to responsibly discharge their obligations, not only to customers and shareholders, but to the communities in which they operated and the environment from which they extracted resources.

But if there is one area where we as believers need to be especially alert and active with respect to preventing and combatting the abuse of freedom, it is with respect to abuses of religious freedom. I am convinced that the greatest threat to religious freedom in our society comes not from the academic challenges to faith from atheists and secularists, but from abuses of religious freedom by religious people themselves. Such abuses provide critics, governments, and other institutions with the public support and justification for actions to suppress or circumscribe all religious thought and expression. By abuses of religious freedom I mean the use of deceit, coercion, and threats and acts of violence to achieve religious ends—as when children, women, or minorities are oppressed in the name of religion; when abortionists or gays or physicians engaged in euthanasia are threatened with violence in the name of religion; or when non-believers and believers of whatever stripe are made the objects of religious vendettas or jihads. None of these tactics are the way of Jesus who never coerced anyone to follow or obey him, but rather invited people to choose to follow and obey by the exercise of their own free will.

Safeguarding Science from Unethical Uses

Suppose one is thoroughly convinced of the merits and benefits of science and is in a position of managing or directing public resources in support of scientific research and development. As believers, acutely conscious of mankind's fallen nature and propensity for evil, do we not also have a special role to play in calling attention to the potentially dark side of science—its application to unethical ends—and the need to safeguard against such applications? Performing such a role should not be presented or seen as "anti-science" but as assisting in the protection of science from applications that discredit it.

Consequently, when I was in Parliament, and later a member of the board of governors of the Canadian Council of Academies, I strongly supported the idea that major science projects—for example, those involved in the study and manipulation of the human genome—should be subject to Economic Environmental Ethical Social Legal (EEESL) studies[5] and constraints. Such studies seek to determine the implications of scientific research and development projects in these areas and propose measures to avoid misuse and mitigate negative consequences.

As a member of the Standing Committee on Health in our Parliament I was also involved in hearings on the application of the latest scientific techniques to assisted human reproduction through enhanced *in vitro* fertilization and stem cell research. This provided an opportunity to address the perennial question as to what extent the state should encourage and support scientific experimentation, the results of which may lead to serious harms as well as benefits. My colleagues and I sought, for example, to have a provision written into Canada's Assisted Human Reproduction Act[6] stipulating that where there was a definable conflict between that which is scientifically possible and that which is ethically preferable, it would be the ethical course of action that would prevail.[7]

Application

You may not be embedded in or involved with an energy company or scientific establishment as referred to above, but

Counter-Transformation of Evil Into Good

you are no doubt embedded in or involved with some organization or institution—a school, a hospital, a union, an interest group, a political party, or a business of some sort—where you are employed.

And if that is the case, could it be that your role as a believer is to be alert to instances in the life and work of that institution where the forces of evil are fastening on to things that are inherently or potentially good and twisting them into something bad? Perhaps it is the pursuit of returns on investment turned into exploitation or environmental degradation, bargaining power morphed into intimidation, communications twisted into the spin and the lie, or the pursuit of organizational efficiency and effectiveness that destroys human relationships, which needs to be explicitly recognized and resisted.

And no matter what our role in society, do not all of us as professing Christians have a responsibility to guard against the abuse of religious freedom, in particular, by the overzealous members of our own faith communities? The psalmist David was discharging this responsibility when, conscious of the "zeal that consumes," he prayed, "May those who hope in you not be disgraced because of me ... ; may those who seek you not be put to shame because of me...."[8]

Let us continue to pray, as Jesus instructed, "Lead us not into temptation, but deliver us from the evil one,"[9] especially the attempts of the evil one to turn even our faith toward means and ends that will discredit the way to God in the eyes of those who so desperately need to find it. Above all, let us seek to become instruments of the grace of God in effecting the counter-transformation of evil into good.

Notes

1. Genesis 50:20
2. Romans 5:20
3. Genesis 45: 4-17; 50:20
4. The Constitution Act, 1982, Schedule B to the Canada Act 1982 (UK), 1982, c 11.
5. Recognition, within the scientific community itself, of the need for such studies arose out of retrospective reflection and regret concerning the ethical implications of the development of nuclear science, which made possible the creation of the atomic bomb. Following the Second World War, the US Department of Energy specifically monitored the genetic implications for persons exposed to nuclear fallout, which in turn led to the project to sequence the human genome. This time provision was made for 5% of the budget of the Human Genome Project to be committed to the Ethical, Legal and Social Implications (ELSI) Research Program to foster basic and applied research on the ethical, legal, and social implications of genetic and genomic research for individuals, families, and communities. It is significant that Dr. Francis Collins, co-director of the Human Genome Project and a strong supporter of such studies, is a practicing Christian. See Francis S. Collins, *The Language of God: A Geneticist Presents Evidence for Belief* (Free Press, 2006).
6. Assisted Human Reproduction Act, S.C. 2004, c.2.
7. Regulating Assisted Human Reproduction and Related Research: Canadian Alliance Minority Report, by Preston Manning, M.P.; Diane Ablonczy, M.P.; Rob Merrifield, M.P.; James Lunney, M.P. December 10, 2001.
8. Psalm 69:6
9. Matthew 6:13

5

The Good and Evil of Bureaucracies

The Scriptures have little to say about the governance and administrative systems of Egypt, Babylonia, and Medo-Persia in which exiles like Joseph, Daniel, and Esther found themselves embedded. But there can be little doubt from the historical accounts of these empires that bureaucratic organization of some sort was a feature of those systems and that dealing with the potential of bureaucracies for both beneficial and malevolent behaviour must have been a constant aspect of the experience of the believing exiles embedded in them.

For example, the administrative machinery over which Joseph presided must have been elaborate and immense in order to collect and store all the grain from Egypt's seven years of good harvests, to redistribute it during the lean years, and, in the process, to systematically establish Pharaoh's ownership and control over virtually all the physical and human resources of Egypt.

With respect to Babylonia, besides a large and formidable army, the administration in which Daniel and his friends came to hold high office included a vast array of satraps, prefects, governors, advisors, treasurers, judges, magistrates, and provincial officials.[1]

And in Medo-Persia, not only did the administration consist of "satraps, governors and nobles of the 127 provinces stretching from India to Cush,"[2] but even the ruler's harem of which Esther became a reluctant member was elaborately and hierarchically organized.[3]

Notwithstanding the potential of the complex military and governmental organizations for doing harm, Joseph, Daniel, and Esther were able to use their positions within them for doing good—in Joseph's case, for the "saving of many lives" from famine;[4] in Daniel's case, for saving the lives of Nebuchadnezzar's many advisors and officials from the uncontrolled fury of their king;[5] and in Esther's case, for saving the lives of her own people from genocide.[6]

Protecting Clients From Bureaucratic Abuse

But now flash forward through the centuries to our day. If you are a believer embedded in a public administration[7] you will often be practising the outworking of your faith in a bureaucratic environment. And if you are a politician and legislator dealing with health, education, social welfare, childcare, senior care, and other related services of the welfare state, bureaucracy will be the principal organizational and delivery mechanism to which you must relate. Such bureaucracies are capable of providing essential and beneficial services to large numbers of people and of achieving much good, but they are also capable of unknowingly and unintentionally doing harm.

Let us, therefore, explore how believers embedded in such organizations, or responsible for their creation and management, can prevent harm and safeguard bureaucratic organizations from their "dark side." That dark side includes the potential to do real harm to those whom bureaucracies are intended to help because of how such organizations transmit information and divide responsibility.

Bureaucracies as Information Systems

My earliest exposure to the nature of bureaucracies occurred in the 1960s while my father was Premier of the Province of Alberta. My thinking on this subject was very much influenced at the time by the doctoral thesis of a friend and colleague, Dr. Erick Schmidt. Erick, a committed Christian, was Secretary to the Executive Council (Cabinet) of the Government of Alberta. Erick's doctoral dissertation was entitled *The Morphology of Bureaucratic Knowledge*.[8]

The Good and Evil of Bureaucracies

His dissertation drew upon much of the classical literature on bureaucracy, on insights based on modern "systems analysis" and cybernetic theory, and on Dr. Schmidt's practical experience with the Alberta government bureaucracy. It analyzed bureaucratic organizations, with their layers and layers of "boxes," each reporting to the box above it, as information systems. These systems transmitted information on people, resources, and situations upward to decision makers, and transmitted decisions, orders, and policy guidelines downward through middle management to front-line workers.

Dr. Schmidt's contention was that these bureaucratic structures transmitted certain types of information accurately, for example, concrete information on things that could be measured and quantified, such as how many barrels of oil were produced per day by Alberta's oil fields. But these same structures could not transmit other types of data accurately at all—for example, subjective data pertaining to values, feelings, emotions, relationships—precisely the information you needed to humanely provide effective services to people, especially people with special needs like the very young, the old, the poor, or the sick.

According to Dr. Schmidt's thesis, not only do bureaucratic information systems have trouble transmitting to decision makers and workers the information they need in order to care humanely and efficiently for people with special needs, but those systems actually filter out much of the required information and substitute other less relevant, even dangerously misleading, information only because it can be objectified and quantified. This is why caring systems, organized in a bureaucratic fashion, not only tend to reduce people to files and numbers but in the extreme can become so inhuman in their functioning that they become a menace rather than a help to the very people they are supposed to serve.

Dr. Schmidt went on to predict specific people-damaging incidents that might occur later in the 1970s to Albertans being served by Alberta's health, education, child-welfare, penal, and social-welfare bureaucracies—incidents that would occur not because of any lack of professionalism or dedication on the part of Alberta's civil servants but because of the nature of bureaucracy itself and its inherent inability to handle people with care. That same decade, a journalist with the *Edmonton Journal*, Wendy Koenig, distinguished herself with a series of reports on precisely the types of incidents that Schmidt had predicted.

The question therefore arises (which I shall attempt to answer in a moment), what can believers embedded in or responsible for the management of such bureaucracies do to avoid or mitigate this potential for harm due to the manner in which bureaucracies process information?

The Good and Evil of Bureaucracies

The Bureaucratic Division of Responsibility

Long before Dr. Schmidt penned his thesis, the great Russian author, Leo Tolstoy, arrived at similar conclusions through artistic and spiritual insights documented in *Resurrection,* the one great novel he wrote after his religious conversion.[9] Prince Nekhlyudov, the hero of the novel and a surrogate for Tolstoy himself, has just witnessed the death from sun-stroke of two political prisoners in the care of the Russian legal and penal system. But he is unable to identify anyone who is "responsible" for what he regards as their murder, other than the system itself which assumes no responsibility. And so he concludes:

> All this happened … because all these people—governors, inspectors, police-officers and policemen—consider that there are circumstances in this world when man owes no humanity to man. Every one of them—Maslennikov (the governor), the inspector, the officer of the escort—if he had not been a governor, an inspector, an officer, would have thought twenty times before sending people off in such heat and such a crowd; they would have stopped twenty times on the way if they had noticed a man getting faint and gasping for breath—they would have got him out of the crowd and into the shade, given him water and allowed him to rest, and then if anything had happened they would have shown some pity. They did nothing of the sort: they even prevented others from

helping; because they were thinking not of human beings and their obligations towards them but of the duties and responsibilities of their office, which they placed above the demands of human relations. That is the whole truth of the matter. If once we admit, be it for a single hour or in a single instance, that there can be anything more important than compassion for a fellow human being, then there is no crime against man that we cannot commit with an easy conscience.[10]

For a number of years I always re-read Tolstoy's *Resurrection* at Easter. But the truth of his observations and their relevance to the operations of bureaucracy in modern times came home to me with particular force while I was doing community development in the Slave Lake region of northern Alberta in the 1970s and became personally aware of what came to be known as the Wabasca Baby tragedy. The facts of this case are as follows.

In April 1973, Joan Belinda Manybears, the three-month-old daughter of Lillian Manybears, became ill of an infection at her home in the aboriginal community of Wabasca, 250 miles north of Edmonton, Alberta. Her mother took the infant to the nursing station in Wabasca where it was recommended that she be transported to the nearest hospital in Slave Lake. An ambulance was summoned to transport Belinda to the Slave Lake Hospital where, upon examination, it was recommended that the ambulance continue on to a hospital in Edmonton.

By the time the driver reached the town of Westlock just north of Edmonton, it was clear that the child was in serious distress. The driver stopped at the Westlock Hospital but, sadly, it was too late and Belinda was pronounced dead. The ambulance driver was then instructed to proceed to the Royal Alexandra Hospital in Edmonton where the provincial coroner was based so that he could perform an autopsy. The autopsy was performed without the permission of the mother and, due to an administrative oversight, without securing the services of a mortician to prepare the body afterward for burial. The body of the child was subsequently placed in a cardboard box and returned to Slave Lake where it was then delivered back to the mother by ambulance with little or no explanation of what had transpired.

Needless to say, the mother was horribly shocked to receive the dead body of her child in this condition and this way. When news of the incident became known, there was a media storm followed by public outrage and demands in the Alberta Legislature for a public inquiry.

The Minister of Health and Social Development at the time, the Hon. Neil Crawford, responded by requesting the Alberta Hospital Services Commission to make inquiries and report regarding the handling of the body of the infant.[11] In July of 1973 the Commission duly reported that all the activities carried out in connection with the incident were "in accordance with accepted standards" and that no particular individual, institution, or procedure could be held responsible for what had happened.[12]

Its chief recommendation was a bureaucratic one, that changes should be made to the applicable regulations, to which the Province responded with a bureaucratic prescription, an Order in Council prescribing ten pages of revisions to the Provincial Board of Health Regulations Respecting Preparation and Transportation of Dead Bodies, Funerals, Interment, and Disinterment.[13]

Once the Wabasca Baby tragedy became the subject of media stories and debate in the Alberta Legislature, dozens of people asked the same question: How could this happen? Couldn't one person in the system—a nurse, a doctor, an administrator, the coroner—have seen what was happening or might happen and intervened so that a grieving mother would not receive the dead body of her child in a cardboard box delivered like a package from FedEx?

The best answer and the clue to the prevention of such atrocities by care-giving bureaucracies is not to be found in the debate in the Alberta Legislature or amendments to the regulations for the handling of dead bodies, but again in Tolstoy's faith-based explanation of such tragedies paraphrased as follows:

All this comes from the fact that all these people, professional and well meaning as they may be—health-service administrators, nurses, doctors, coroners, ambulance dispatchers, and drivers—are placed in circumstances where human relations are not necessary between human beings. All these functionaries were obliged to think, not first and foremost of a mother and child and their duty toward them but rather of the requirements of the positions they held.... It is only necessary that people should hold bureaucratic positions; that they should be persuaded that there is a kind of business called government service which allows people to treat other people as things without having human brotherly relations with them; and that they should be so linked together by this government service that the responsibility for the results of their deeds should not fall on any one of them individually. Without these conditions, human tragedies like this would be impossible in our times. It all lies in the fact that people think there are circumstances in which one may deal with human beings without love.[14]

Application to Your Situation

If you are a believer living in this society hostile to your faith and embedded by the providential guidance of God in a bureaucratic system—particularly a public-service bureaucracy ostensibly dedicated to providing essential services to needy people—perhaps you are there to help protect that bureaucracy from its dark side and ensure that it functions as an instrument for good rather than as a source of unintended harms.

Consider, therefore, what you can do to perform that role to the best of your God-given ability and strength, your starting point being to pray for the wisdom and prophetic insight required to better understand the organization in which you are embedded; to perceive the nature of bureaucratic systems from a spiritual perspective as did Schmidt and Tolstoy; and to resolve to be vigilant in guarding your bureaucracy against its dark side. I will say more on how to safeguard bureaucracies from inadvertently doing harm in the next chapter.

Notes

1. Daniel 3:2; 6:1-3
2. Esther 8: 9
3. Esther 2:8-9
4. Genesis 47:13-25; 50:19-20
5. Daniel 2:24
6. Esther 8:1-13
7. While my focus in this chapter is on the potential of public (government) bureaucracies for good and evil, many of the observations made and measures recommended for mitigating the bad and facilitating the good are equally applicable to private-sector bureaucracies such as are to be found in large corporations and NGOs.
8. *The Morphology of Bureaucratic Knowledge*, University of Alberta, Department of Sociology, doctoral dissertation by Erick Schmidt dated August 1, 1975.
9. Leo Tolstoy, *Resurrection* (Penguin Books, 1983).
10. Ibid., p. 447-8
11. The Commission was directed to ascertain the following: (1) What treatment services were provided at Slave Lake, Edmonton, or elsewhere, to the infant child from, on or about the 16th of April, 1973, until her death? (2) Following the death of the infant child, whether the conduct of persons responsible for handling the dead body was in accordance with the existing standards of conduct in the Province of Alberta. (3) Whether in the opinion of the Alberta Hospital Services Commission existing standards of conduct in the Province of Alberta conform with a contemporary sense of propriety and respect for the deceased.

Notes, *continued*

12. In particular, the Commission reported on July 25th, 1973:

    - That the activities and procedures carried out by the hospitals and staff members were in accordance with accepted standards in Alberta.
    - That the conduct of persons responsible for handling the dead body was in accordance with the existing standards of conduct in the Province of Alberta.
    - That the body was handled properly in that it was placed in a new container which is manufactured and recognized as being "purpose designed" for the temporary transportation of small bodies.

13. It states, "that the Provincial Board of Health Regulations, Division 26, Regulations Relating to Funerals and to the Preparation of Dead Bodies for Interment, Cremation, and Transportation be reviewed and clarified, in particular that section 26-5-5 be made more explicit and designate the levels of responsibility as they apply to health-care facilities, morticians, or relatives claiming bodies."

14. P. Manning paraphrase of Leo Tolstoy, *Resurrection* (Penguin Books, 1983), p.447-8.

6

Safeguarding Public Bureaucracies From Doing Harm

We have previously observed that the working environment for Joseph, Daniel, and Esther—believers in exile in foreign and hostile environments—was that of the huge and bureaucratic administrations which characterized the governing structures of the great empires of Egypt, Babylon, and Medo-Persia. We noted that such organizations have potential for doing both good and evil and that the exiles played an important role in promoting the good and constraining the evil. That in turn led us to examine, from a spiritual perspective, the positive and the "dark" sides of the large public bureaucracies of today and the opportunities and obligations of believers embedded therein to enhance their potential for good and to safeguard them from their potential for harm.

Let us now examine the measures that are available to us to prevent well-intended public-service bureaucracies from doing harm—to prevent evil from arising from good. I see this safeguarding, especially by believers embedded in such systems, as essentially a spiritual undertaking, cooperating with the work of God in "delivering us from evil."

Antidotes and Preventative Measures

Are there antidotes to the vulnerabilities and predispositions of bureaucratic organizations to do harm, measures that those in positions to direct or safeguard bureaucratic operations can employ and that believers in such positions should champion and practise? My experiences with bureaucracies, particularly as a Christian believer, management consultant, and legislator, suggest the following.

> *1. Be reluctant to consign, without reservation or the consideration of alternatives, the care of human beings to bureaucracies.*

As Christians, instructed by our Lord to personally and collectively care for the poor, the sick, the lonely, and the oppressed[1] we should be reluctant in the first place to assign, without reservation or the serious consideration of alternatives, the care of human beings, especially vulnerable human beings, to state-run social welfare bureaucracies. When we see injured human beings lying by the side of life's road, Jesus' instruction to us is to follow the example of the Good

Safeguarding Public Bureaucracies From Doing Harm

Samaritan who first of all offered personal attention and care,[2] rather than defaulting to the position of "let the state take care of them."

At one time, of course, the Christian church was the primary institution in many countries, including Canada, for providing care to the most needy members of society. In modern times that function has been transferred, to a large extent, to the state. While there are certainly benefits to that transfer and it is unlikely ever to be reversed, as believers we need to be more constantly and personally proactive on the front lines of social service—offering alternative, more personalized care as individuals, families, churches, NGOs, and social enterprises whose care commitment is rooted in the life and teachings of Jesus.

As legislators, supportive of public service bureaucracies but sensitive to their dark side, before we automatically assign the care of any vulnerable class of persons to large, impersonal care systems, we ought first to inquire whether or not there are smaller, more personal, and more humane care-giving alternatives and how these might be given greater opportunity and resources to provide that care.[3]

For example, as our population ages and special care for the old and dying becomes an urgent priority, the creation and support of end-of-life home care and community-based hospice care programs and facilities by faith-based and other local groups should be encouraged, not prevented by public policy and social legislation. Such programs and facilities are especially required as alternatives to people dying in large and impersonal health-care facilities where the beds are urgently needed for others and where physician-assisted suicide is now sanctioned by Canadian law.

2. Bring the top to the bottom.

An increasing number of private-sector service organizations are requiring top and middle managers to spend more time "on the front lines" where they must meet face to face with real customers and share the experiences of frontline workers. Therefore, let us strongly encourage,[4] even compel, the top and middle management of social welfare bureaucracies to regularly and substantially meet with their frontline employees and their clients so as to receive firsthand information and awareness of needs and conditions which will never be accurately transmitted through bureaucratic information channels.

3. Respect and encourage the exercise of freedom of conscience by bureaucratic caregivers.

If we are going to ask those embedded in bureaucratic care systems to be more humane and relational in their conduct and delivery of services, then we need to give them more freedom to follow the dictates of their own consciences—those inner compasses which, if spiritually sensitive, alert us to evil and draw us toward the good.

In drafting legislation establishing, supporting, or modifying public services delivered by bureaucracies, explicit attention should be given to the inclusion of "conscience" or "non-participation" rights[5] which entitle public employees, for reasons of conscience, to refrain from participating in ethically questionable activities that employment by that bureaucracy may otherwise dictate.[6] It is true that such provisions will raise supervisory and equity problems for the managers of such services and the courts. But accepting and dealing with such problems is preferable to denying those employed by public bureaucracies, especially frontline workers, their rights to freedom of religion, conscience, thought, belief, opinion, and expression as guaranteed by the Charter of Rights and Freedoms.

4. *Encourage greater freedom of action for bureaucratic caregivers.*

Saying that we respect and encourage freedom of conscience if we do not also permit and encourage people to act according to their consciences is hypocritical and a contradiction in terms.[7] For frontline workers employed by bureaucracies, there is a need to provide more room for

Leadership Lessons from the Lives of the Exiles

them to "step outside" their bureaucratic role from time to time in order to follow the dictates of their consciences and to act humanely rather than bureaucratically toward those in their care.

I realize of course that encouraging such independent behaviour on the part of bureaucrats can again create a major challenge for supervisors and can be open to abuse (more on how to curtail abuse in a moment). But I am prompted to encourage such allowances nonetheless as a result of experiences like the following.

Back when I was in the management consulting business, our firm was engaged to conduct a socio-economic impact assessment of a heavy oil plant being proposed by Imperial Oil for construction in the Cold Lake area of northeast Alberta. Our assignment was to assess the potential impact of the proposed plant on seven Aboriginal bands in the area (six Cree bands and one Chipewyan) and to propose measures to mitigate negative impacts and maximize potential benefits.

I had some experience with Cree bands and personally knew some of the Cree band leaders in the area. But I needed someone to improve my understanding of the Chipewyan people. Knowing of my need, a friend introduced me to a Métis woman, part Chipewyan, named Ernestine Gibot. Ernestine advised me about the Cold Lake Chipewyans and

Safeguarding Public Bureaucracies From Doing Harm

eventually became a good friend—the best aboriginal friend I ever had. As she opened up about her own life, including her spiritual beliefs, she gave me new insights into the operations of the ubiquitous social welfare system that Canada has established for its aboriginal people.

This is not the place to tell Ernestine's lengthy and heart-wrenching story in detail, but the following aspects of it are relevant to this commentary on the nature of bureaucracies and how to render them more beneficial to those they are intended to serve.[8]

At the age of forty-nine, with little formal education, no money, no friends at hand, no experience of city living or employment, and a drinking problem, Ernestine decided to leave her life in the northern Alberta bush as the abused wife of a Métis trapper and "start over" in the large and strange city of Edmonton.

It then took seven years of wandering around within the bureaucratic maze of services available to aboriginal people in Edmonton, between when Ernestine first arrived and when she got a self-sustaining job, first as a "consultant" with our firm and soon after as a teacher's aide in an inner city school.

The path Ernestine followed took her to such agencies and destinations as the Charles Camsel Hospital; Poundmaker Lodge (an alcoholism treatment centre); provincial and city welfare offices; the Department of Indian Affairs; Hilltop House (a residence for Indian women); numerous bars, hotels, and liquor stores; the Court House; the city jail; several Catholic churches; the Edmonton Housing Authority; the Native Friendship Centre; the Alberta Native Communications Society; the Native Counselling Service; and the Alberta Vocational College.

By retracing Ernestine's steps and discussing them with her, I learned four things about the nature of the complex network of bureaucratic "helping systems" established to serve Canadian aboriginals:

- That sometimes it delivered certain services effectively—in particular health care and occasionally emergency financial support, accommodation, and training.

- That at the same time it failed to provide guidance at critical times, or to offer encouragement, incentive, and meaningful links to employers.

- That the few individuals within the system who actually helped Ernestine were individuals she would not have met had she not been "in the system."

- And most importantly, that in order to truly help Ernestine, these individuals often had to step outside their professional roles and act on

> their own initiative, rendering services above and beyond those called for by their job descriptions and sometimes in violation of the system's rules.

This was the case, for example, with her doctor and her priest who told her, "We shouldn't really be saying this, but you must leave the north and leave your husband or you'll be dead within a year." It was also the case with two social workers who treated Ernestine as a friend, meeting with her "after hours" and against regulations rather than simply treating her as a client. And it was the case with the employment counsellor who referred Ernestine to me, even when our firm was not on the agency's approved list of potential employers. (After all, what management consulting firm would possibly hire a mid-fifties aboriginal woman with a Grade 4 education?)

It is experiences like this which led me to address the question of what can be done to shorten the tortuous path through the bureaucratic maze that the Ernestines of our country must travel to escape the ravages of their past. It is experiences like this that lead me to encourage greater freedom of action for frontline caregivers employed by bureaucracies and responsible for serving those Ernestines.

5. *Accept greater responsibility and accountability for the exercise of your freedom of conscience and action.*

With greater freedom must come a greater acceptance of accountability and responsibility. Hence policy, legislation, and regulations allowing for the exercise of greater freedom of conscience and action by frontline caregivers employed by bureaucracies must be accompanied by the provision of mechanisms to ensure greater accountability and acceptance of responsibility for outcomes.

In the private sector, these include the requirement of independent audits of corporate performance (not only financial audits but, increasingly, social and environmental audits), the institution of whistle-blowing mechanisms within companies to facilitate the reporting of illegal or unethical actions, and the provision of financial liability and penalties for deliberate or inadvertent actions that injure others.

Would there not be merit, therefore, in strengthening and broadening the audit requirements for public service bureaucracies and unions to include social as well as financial audits? Would there not be merit in expanding and strengthening the provision of whistle-blowing legislation and mechanisms to public bureaucracies and public service unions, just as such safeguards were instituted in greater measure following the gross violations of marketplace freedoms by corporations leading to the financial melt down of 2008?[9] And would there not be merit in partially and selectively withdrawing the immunity of the Crown and public servants from legal action when their activities and those of public agencies do demonstrable harm to citizens and their interests?[10]

Application to Your Situation

If you are a Christian believer embedded in a bureaucracy of any kind, could it be that you are there in part to provide an understanding of the nature of bureaucratic systems from a spiritual perspective—serving to protect that bureaucracy from the inadvertent expression of its dark side and to enhance its potential for good?

Suppose you are a believer providentially embedded in a government as a legislator, policy maker, or administrator, operating in a society hostile to your faith but challenged to meet the needs of some vulnerable segment of society. Could it be that you personally are there by divine appointment:

- To insist that other care-giving alternatives be considered before automatically consigning persons in need to large, impersonal, bureaucratic care systems?

- To provide leadership by example through your willingness to frequently visit the "front lines" and expose yourself to the conditions and experience of frontline workers and those whom they serve?

Leadership Lessons from the Lives of the Exiles

- To be that ethical salt and light of which Jesus spoke; to listen to that still small voice of your spiritually sensitized conscience and to follow its dictates?
- To personally accept responsibility for some of the outcomes of the bureaucracy's operations for which the bureaucracy itself will rarely accept responsibility, even at personal cost to your reputation, income, and career?

Will you do so even if that leads to opting out of some unethical activity and risking a career-limiting clash with the self-serving ethics of the system? Are you even willing and prepared on occasion to "step outside" your job description and system role to relate to some needy person on a personal and human level, as dealing with a neighbour bearing the image of God, rather than as a "client" or a mere name in a file for which you have a statutory obligation?

In recognizing and accepting such perspectives, roles, and responsibilities as believers in exile within bureaucratic systems, my prayer would be that we be conscious—as I believe that Joseph, Daniel, and Esther were conscious—that we are called to such positions by the God whom we serve. If so, our role is to join with him in ensuring that harm is prevented and good prevails, to the benefit and "saving" of many lives.

Notes

1. Matthew 25: 31-46
2. Luke 10:25-37
3. The Canadian Constitution assigns to the provinces responsibilities for "The Establishment, Maintenance, and Management of Hospitals, Asylums, Charities, and Eleemosynary Institutions in and for the Province ...." (BNA 1867 91 (7). Note that "eleemosynary" is an old word literally meaning "almsgiving," the same word used by Jesus in his Sermon on the Mount (Matthew 6:1-2 KJV). But since most Canadian charities want the right to issue tax-deductible receipts for charitable donations, it is the federal government, specifically the Canada Revenue Agency, which has largely assumed responsibility for defining and regulating Canada's charitable sector. Federal laws governing charities are long overdue for a complete overhaul, as has been done in the United Kingdom, separating the definition and regulation of charity from the federal finance department and expanding the capacities of charities including religious institutions, for example, through facilitating the formation of social enterprises and the use of social impact bonds.
4. Exhortations for Christians to behave in this way are to be found, for example, in Paul's description of our "calling" in Ephesians 2 and the example of Jesus found in Philippians 2:5-11.
5. For example, private member's bills have been introduced in several provincial legislatures which would prohibit an employer from refusing to hire, advance, or promote, or to threaten, discipline, or dismiss a health-care professional because the health-care professional is not willing to take part in or to counsel any health-care procedure that offends a tenet of the health professional's religion or the belief of the health

Notes, *continued*

professional that human life is sacred. See http://www.assembly. ab.ca/ISYS/LADDAR_files/docs/bills/bill/legislature_24/ session_4/20000217_bill-212.pdf (accessed August 19, 2015).

In the federal Parliament, similar private member's bills have also been introduced which would criminalize the coercion of health-care practitioners into taking part in medical procedures that offend the practitioner's religion or belief that human life is inviolable. See http://www.parl.gc.ca/HousePublications/ Publication.aspx?Language=E&Mode=1&DocId=2333614 (accessed August 19, 2015).

For a related discussion of "conscience rights' in relation to euthanasia and physician assisted suicide, see the factum (pages 5-7) of The Christian Medical and Dental Society of Canada and The Canadian Federation of Catholic Physicians' Societies in the 2014 Carter (assisted suicide) Supreme Court of Canada hearing: http:// www.scc-csc.gc.ca/WebDocuments-DocumentsWeb/35591/ FM120_Internener_Christian-Medical-Dental-Society_and_ Catholic-Physician-Societes.pdf (accessed August 19, 2015).

6. In Canada the case for allowing "conscience rights" to be recognized and enforced in particular legislation would appear to be strongest when it rests on linking conscience to explicit religious beliefs, protected by the Charter, and being able to demonstrate the sincerity with which the adherent holds and practises those beliefs. See the Supreme Court of Canada decision in Syndicate Northcrest v. Amselem 2004 SCC 47, in dissent, Bastarache J. , (LeBel, and Deschamps JJ concurring).

7. I once encountered this contradiction in a conversation with a senior official of the Chinese Communist Party when I drew her attention to the obvious contradiction between provisions in

Notes, *continued*

the Chinese constitution guaranteeing freedom of conscience and belief while the government continued to suppress religious expression and activity. She replied, without apparently seeing any contradiction in her reply, "In this area, the Chinese people are free to believe whatever they want; they just can't talk about it or act upon it."

8. Ernestine Gibot's story has been well told by Robert Collins, former editor of the Imperial Oil Review, in, "The Long Hard Road of Ernestine Gibot," *Reader's Digest* (October 1984).

9. In 2002, a private member's bill was introduced in the Canadian House of Commons entitled The Whistle Blower Human Rights Act, which would "respect the protection of employees in the public service who make allegations in good faith respecting wrongdoing in the public service." It failed to pass but was followed in 2005 by the passage of the Public Servants Disclosure Protection Act (S.C. 2005, c. 46) which is now law and forms the basis of federal whistle-blowing protection. Provincially, all jurisdictions except British Columbia, Newfoundland, and Prince Edward Island have some form of whistle-blowing legislation in place. In the US, section 806 of the Sarbanes Oxley Act contains significant protection and support for corporate whistle-blowers—these provisions generally being stronger and more far-reaching than those provided by Canadian legislation.

10. For a recent analysis of this issue see http://lawreformcommission.sk.ca/Crown_Immunity_Report.pdf (accessed August 19, 2015). This is a 2013 Report of the Saskatchewan Law Reform Commission re: clarifying and modifying the law concerning Crown immunity. In this Report (page 8) the authors note, "Many

Notes, *continued*

observers agree that a rule of construction that presumes immunity for the Crown is broader than necessary to meet the objective of governing effectively. Particular concern has been raised that the doctrine's continued operation cannot be reconciled with the expanded role of the Crown.... As Dickson C.J. wrote for the majority of the Supreme Court of Canada in 1983: 'The doctrine of Crown immunity seems to conflict with basic notions of equality before the law. The more active the government becomes in activities that had once been considered the preserve of private persons, the less easy it is to understand why the Crown need be, or ought to be, in a position different from the subject.' "

7

Diligence and Excellence

Joseph, Daniel, and Esther were believers living in exile in societies, political systems, and bureaucracies hostile to their faith who nevertheless came to occupy high political offices and render exceptional public service. So what were the characteristics of their lives that stand out as most essential to:

- The retention and deepening of their faith under such circumstances?

- Their influence and effectiveness as leaders under such circumstances?

My principal conclusions are that it was their diligence in adhering to certain spiritual practices that was highly instrumental in preserving their faith and that it was their God-given and God-directed commitment to excellence in service that made them so effective and influential. These conclusions then lead me to ask:

- How diligent are we, as believers living in societies hostile to our faith, in attending to those spiritual practices and disciplines that will preserve and deepen it?

- How committed are we to equipping ourselves to serve with excellence in positions of public service in societies and situations indifferent or hostile to our faith commitments?

In raising and addressing these questions I do not mean to imply that we can maintain our spirituality or achieve excellence in God's service by our own efforts alone. Surely it is God himself who is active in preserving and strengthening the faith of those he has positioned in faith-testing situations and it is he who ultimately equips us for excellence in service under such circumstances. But at the same time we need to do our part—to avail ourselves of those means which he has provided to maintain and strengthen our relationship with himself and to serve with excellence in whatever position he has chosen for us.[1]

Diligence

It would appear from the scriptural record that Daniel and his companions were consistently faithful and diligent in their adherence to certain spiritual practices—prayer,

Diligence and Excellence

fellowship with one another as believers, and the dietary requirements of the Mosaic law—despite enormous cultural and political pressures to abandon such practices for those more acceptable to their Babylonian peers and superiors.

While still teenagers, Daniel and his companions were forcibly enrolled in a three-year program to immerse them in the language and literature of the Babylonians. At the completion of this program they were to be examined by the king himself as to whether they were fit to enter his service. Then as now, "you are what you eat" is true both physically and intellectually. Daniel and his companions resolved not to defile themselves with the king's food and wine, perhaps also symbolic in their minds of not defiling themselves with the products and intoxicants of a pagan culture. They persuaded the king's officials to make their diet and its impact upon them the test of their worthiness for continued education and service. They passed the test with flying colors, preserving and strengthening their spiritual identity in a strange and hostile cultural environment by diligently adhering to the dietary provisions of the Mosaic law.[2]

Some time later, Daniel's companions again risked their very lives by their diligent adherence to the first and second of the Ten Commandments.[3] They refused, even upon the threat of being thrown into a fiery furnace, to bow down to and worship the golden statue that Nebuchadnezzar had erected on the plains of Dura.[4] They refused to have any other gods before Jehovah and they refused to bow down to or worship any idol.

Daniel and his companions were especially diligent in maintaining their prayer life. They prayed together for the wisdom required by Daniel to interpret Nebuchadnezzar's dreams.[5] Daniel himself developed a spiritual practice that he apparently followed no matter what regime he was serving and what restrictions it placed on religious worship.[6] When faced with a law forbidding the worship of anyone but King Darius, "… he went home to his upstairs room where the windows opened toward Jerusalem. Three times a day he got down on his knees and prayed, giving thanks to his God, just as he had done before."[7]

In the case of Esther, her diligence took the form of faithful and consistent adherence to the inspired advice of her spiritual and political mentor Mordecai, even to the point where such adherence endangered her position and life.[8]

In the case of Joseph, Scripture tells us nothing about his spiritual practices in Egypt. Yet after years of immersion in the Egyptian political and religious system he demonstrated in later life greater understanding of the purposes and ways of God than his brothers who had never physically departed from the household of faith. Whatever spiritual disciplines Joseph practised they must have been learned at an early age before he was sold into slavery in Egypt. Perhaps, ironically, his faith was more vigorous than his brothers' precisely because of how it was tested and tried in a hostile environment while theirs remained a "hothouse" faith.

What About Us?

For many of us, even if we have been raised in professing Christian homes and environments, our spiritual practices, after making an initial commitment to follow Jesus, can easily dissipate into little more than sporadic Bible reading, sporadic prayer (mainly at meals), and sporadic church or fellowship-group attendance, punctuated with occasional intensifications when trouble of some sort—health, financial, marital, etc.—drives us back to God.

But such nominal religious practices are simply not adequate to sustain us under any kind of prolonged testing in a hostile spiritual environment. They are certainly not adequate to sustain our presence as "salt and light" at the interface of faith and modern-day business, science, media, politics, or culture.

In an earlier volume of this series on the life of David, we noted the constant attention David gave to his inner life as reflected in the Psalms. And at the risk of repetition, I cannot stress emphatically enough for those endeavouring to live out their faith in hostile cultural environments, especially hostile political environments, the importance of disciplined and diligent attention to:

- *Solitude* as an antidote to constantly being in the public eye and under media scrutiny.

- The practice of *Lectio Divina* as a counter balance to reading or viewing hundreds of pages a week of secular material.[9]

- *Prayer* as an alternative to the incessant communications buzz of media-dominated political discourse.

- *Honouring the body* as a counterbalance to the intense physical and time demands of public life.

- *Self-examination*, including the *examen of consciousness and conscience*, as a counterbalance to the preoccupation of image politics with manufactured and artificial appearances.

- *Spiritual discernment* as an alternative to perceiving and analyzing issues and problems solely from a secular and temporal standpoint.

- *Sabbath Observance*, as a means of establishing a disciplined balance between work and rest, including "turning off" the technological devices and media that so dominate the lives of those in the public arena.

- Integration of all the above into a *Rule* or *Rhythm*

of Life distinctly different from the rhythm of contemporary political life.

Excellence

The scriptural record leaves very little doubt that, despite many distractions and obstacles, Joseph, Daniel, and Esther were very, very good at the political and administrative work they were positioned and called upon to do. For example, if outside auditors had been called in to perform third-party evaluations on Joseph's service to Potiphar, his management of the prison, and his organization and management of the great Egyptian Grain Exchange, their report would have read that he does all these things "excellently."[10] The scriptural interpretation was that "the Lord was with Joseph and gave him success in whatever he did."[11]

Likewise in the case of Esther, it was not only her beauty but also the shrewdness and excellence of her conduct under the guidance of Mordecai that made her the most politically influential member of King Xerxes' harem.[12]

Daniel also performed so excellently that he was constantly promoted over his Babylonian peers to the point where the only grounds that they could find for attacking him and his service was on the basis of his faith.[13]

What About Us?

As believers, especially those of us embedded in political

organizations and systems indifferent or hostile to our faith, are we "excellent" at what we do? Do others see us as exceptional and excellent performers? Through diligence in our spiritual practices, do we consciously and faithfully seek God's wisdom and guidance to enable us to do our work excellently? If the performance auditors were to interview our peers, would they grudgingly be obliged to say, "He/she holds certain religious views and engages in religious practices I don't understand or agree with, but I must admit he/she is very, very good at...."?

If we are in political or public administration positions, is this the reputation we have—a reputation for excellence in public service? And if not, why not?

As a founder of several political parties and as a member of the Canadian Parliament, I became convinced that very few of us in the partisan political arena have undergone the kind of rigorous preparation and training that is required to do our jobs "excellently." To become a barista at a Starbucks coffee bar, one is required to take more than twenty hours of training. But one can become a lawmaker in Canada's Parliament or any of our legislatures without one hour of training in lawmaking. One can become an "elected representative of the people" in any of our democratic assemblies, including our municipal councils, without one hour of preparation or training in what "democratic representation" really involves. How can such lack of preparation possibly result in "excellence" with respect to legislating or democratic representation, let alone policy-making or public administration?

Since I left Parliament, my friends and I have therefore established several organizations and training programs[14] for strengthening the knowledge, skills, ethics, communications capacities, and leadership skills of participants in Canada's political processes, especially those with whom we have some ideological rapport and influence. While this is not the place to elaborate on these organizations or programs, the main point I wish to make is that it is especially important for those of us entering the political arena with a Christian commitment to undertake such preparation and training, including training in how to navigate the faith-political interface wisely and graciously. Why? So that whatever public service we may have opportunity to render, it will be judged by our Lord, our peers, and our fellow citizens as "excellent" and a credit, not a discredit, to our faith in Christ.

Notes

1. As the Apostle Paul reminded the early Christians (believers embedded in the hostile cultures of their day), leaders in God's kingdom are called upon and equipped to "govern diligently" (Romans 12:8) and to both think and practise whatever is true, noble, right, pure, lovely, admirable, praiseworthy, and "excellent" (Philippians 4:8-9).
2. Daniel 1:3-21
3. Exodus 20:3-5
4. Daniel 3
5. Daniel 2:17-18
6. Daniel served in high office under the Babylonian Nebuchadnezzar, Belshazzar his successor, Darius the Mede, and Cyrus the Persian.
7. Daniel 6:10
8. Esther 2:10-11, 20, 22; 4:1-17
9. The purpose is to encounter God through the Scriptures via regular preparation (Silencio); reading short select passages (Lectio); personally reflecting on the application of the passage to oneself (Meditatio); responding to God based on what one has read and encountered (Oratio); resting in the word one has received (Contemplatio); and finally, resolving to act and live out the word received in the place where God has planted us (Incarnatio).
10. Genesis 39:2-6; 21-23; 41:38-43
11. Genesis 39:23
12. Esther 5:1-3; 8:1-3
13. Daniel 6:1-5

Notes, *continued*

14. For more information on these organizations and programs, visit www.manningfoundation.org and www.manningcentre.ca. Of particular interest might be our seminars on Navigating the Faith-Political Interface and Lessons from Wilberforce on the conduct of advocacy campaigns with moral dimensions.

8

Cooperation and Compromise

Believers in exile such as Joseph, Daniel, and Esther—embedded in political systems and societies hostile to their faith yet effective in their political roles—must have had to integrate to some extent with those foreign cultures and cooperate in many respects with the political systems in which they served. At the same time they remained faithful to God and did not cross the line where cooperation becomes compromise and the starting point of unfaithfulness and spiritual decline. So what can we—believers embedded today in cultures and organizations indifferent or hostile to our faith, especially those of us operating at the interface of faith and modern day politics—learn from their experience? To what extent can we cooperate in order to be effective and influential for good? And what are the convictions and practices to which we must hold without compromise if we wish to retain our spiritual identity and a right relationship with God?

Of course it must be recognized that Joseph, Daniel, and Esther were literally "enslaved" in Egypt, Babylon, and Medo-Persia. So one might argue that they had little choice but to integrate and co-operate to a very large extent with the dictates of the cultures, laws, and rulers of those nations. Nevertheless it is worth noting the particulars of their integration and cooperation as specifically mentioned in Scripture, so that we can compare and contrast them with the particulars on which they refused to cooperate or to be compromised.

Cooperation in Egypt

In the case of Joseph, he fit in so well with the household of Potiphar and the administration of the prison in which he was unjustly incarcerated that in each instance he was entrusted with more and more managerial responsibilities. Eventually he even won the confidence of Egypt's supreme ruler through correctly interpreting Pharaoh's dream and prescribing a policy to cope with the famine that it prophesied. Pharaoh then rewarded him by putting him "in charge of the whole land of Egypt"[1] and giving him the Egyptian name Zaphenath-Paneah. He also provided him with an Egyptian wife, Asenath, the daughter of a priest of On (the Egyptian centre of sun worship)[2] with whom he had two sons.

By the time Joseph re-established contact with his brothers, he dressed like an Egyptian, spoke like an Egyptian, had an

Egyptian family, and acted so much like an Egyptian that they failed to recognize him as either a Hebrew or a member of their family. On the basis of all external appearances, an outside observer might well have concluded that Joseph had allowed himself to be completely assimilated by the Egyptian culture and political system, in the process losing virtually all of the distinctives which would have marked him as a God-honouring member of the household of faith.

Cooperation in Babylon

In the case of Daniel and his friends, they were specifically enrolled as impressionable teenagers in a three-year educational program designed to immerse them in the language, traditions, and practices of their Babylonian captors. At the end of their training they were interrogated by the king himself to determine whether they were fit for royal service. The fact that they not only completed this training but also passed the exam with flying colors would indicate that they must have absorbed and mastered a great deal of the culture and politics of Babylon at an early age.[3] Note also that at the very beginning of their training they were given Babylonian names—the message no doubt being, "You are no longer Jews; you are Babylonians now."[4] Daniel in particular was given the name Belteshazzar, which may have been particularly offensive to him since it was the name of Nebuchadnezzar's god.[5]

According to Scripture, Daniel and his friends were, for the most part, successful in managing their relations with Babylonian rulers and in administering the public affairs and offices for which they were made responsible.[6] Successful management and administration in such situations requires a solid understanding of and identification with the political, bureaucratic, and cultural milieu in which one is operating. It also requires a willingness and ability to work cooperatively with subordinates, peers, and superiors. These Jewish exiles distinguished themselves from Babylonian and other foreign functionaries by the excellence of their public service. So thoroughly had Daniel and his compatriots adapted to the society and government of which they had become a part that, apart from their faith, it appears unlikely that an outside observer would have found much to distinguish them from their public service colleagues.

Cooperation in Medo-Persia

The orphan exile Esther rose to the position of Queen of the Medes and Persians. Of all the exiles, it is she who carries "cooperation" with her captors to the greatest extent, for the ultimate purpose, unknown to her at the beginning, of rescuing her people from genocide. Not only is Esther an orphan and an exile in captivity, but she is a woman at a time and in a culture where women are treated as the property of men.

When King Xerxes dethrones and banishes Queen Vashti for defying his authority, his nobles propose an elaborate beauty contest to select her replacement. Esther is enrolled by her uncle Mordecai and wins the favour and approval of everyone she encounters, including the king himself, who selects her as his new queen.[7]

To attain this position, Esther had to completely and utterly subordinate herself to the mores and dictates of the culture, the kingdom, and the harem. As an exile and a woman she has no choice. Rather than being instructed by Mordecai to retain or display her identity as one of God's people, he orders her to keep her Jewish identity a secret. Of all the prominent exiles in Scripture Esther is the one most totally absorbed into the foreign culture in which she finds herself.

Where to Draw the Line Between Cooperation and Compromise

Where and how to "draw the line" between cooperation and compromise is of course a highly relevant issue for Christian believers embedded today in political and governmental institutions unsympathetic to our faith.[8] In fact there are still many Christians who do not believe it is possible to occupy such positions *without* compromising one's faith. Hence they refrain from involvement in politics and government altogether and are highly suspicious and critical of professing Christians who do.

So, where and how did these believers in exile "draw the line" between integrating with the hostile foreign environment in which they found themselves embedded, and compromising their faith and relationship to God?

Five Major Examples from the Exiles' Experience

1. Worship of the One True God

Daniel and his fellow exiles drew the line with respect to the object of their religious worship. They refused, at the risk of their lives, to forsake the worship of the one true God; they refused to bow down in worship or to direct their prayers to an earthly king. In particular, they refused to worship the state when it sought to claim the total allegiance of their minds and hearts.

Shadrach, Meshach, and Abednego, when ordered to bow down and worship the golden image of Nebuchadnezzar on the plains of Dura, simply refused, even when the King threatened to throw them into a fiery furnace. Their refusal was expressed in polite but emphatic terms and contains a declaration of faith in God's ability to deliver them notwithstanding their uncertainty as to whether he would actually do so:

> "O Nebuchadnezzar, we do not need to defend ourselves before you in this matter. If we are thrown into the blazing furnace, the God we serve is able to save us from it, and he will rescue us from your hand, O king. But even if he does not, we want you to know, O king, that we will not serve your gods or worship the image of gold you have set up."[9]

When they were miraculously delivered from the fiery furnace, they earned this testimony regarding where they drew the line from no less than King Nebuchadnezzar himself:

> They trusted in him (their God) and defied the king's command and were willing to give up their lives rather than serve or worship any god except their own God.[10]

Some time later, when Babylon was overthrown by the Medes and Persians, King Darius the Mede was persuaded to issue and enforce an edict "that anyone who prays to any god or man during the next thirty days, except to you, O king, shall be thrown into the lions' den."[11]

And what did Daniel do, even though he held a high position in Darius's administration and was well aware of the decree? "He went home to his upstairs room where the windows opened toward Jerusalem. Three times a day he got down on his knees and prayed, giving thanks to his God, just as he had done before."[12]

Daniel was subsequently thrown into the den of lions but his life was miraculously preserved. And his "drawing of the line" with respect to worship and his ultimate allegiances prompted another decree from Darius, "that in every part of my kingdom people must reverence and fear the God of Daniel."[13]

2. Faith in the Sovereignty of God

Whatever else the exiles had to surrender, they never surrendered their faith in the sovereignty of God—their belief that in the final analysis God was sovereign over their lives, their circumstances, and the kingdoms and political systems in which they were embedded.

Joseph, for example, clung to this belief throughout his trials as a slave and a prisoner when it would have been easy for him to succumb to the idea that God, like his own faith-based family, had abandoned him. He affirmed this belief in the sovereignty of God, even when he was a public official ostensibly under the sovereignty of Pharaoh, telling his brothers, "It was not you who sent me here, but God. He made me father to Pharaoh ... (and) has made me lord of all Egypt."[14] Note that he attributes his political ascendancy to

God and not to Pharaoh.

Likewise Daniel, while serving as an advisor to and servant of one of the most violent, unpredictable, and self-centered rulers of the ancient world—Nebuchadnezzar of Babylon—does not hesitate to declare his belief in the sovereignty of God over human affairs. He declares to the king himself, "… the Most High is sovereign over the kingdoms of men and gives them to anyone he wishes."[15]

3. *Personal Moral Standards*

In the case of Joseph, he refused to compromise his personal integrity and moral standards by succumbing to the sexual temptations of Potiphar's wife. Notwithstanding the sexual mores of Egypt and his master's wife, this is where he chose to draw the line—a refusal to compromise, which cost him dearly, as her false accusations then resulted in the loss of his position and imprisonment.[16]

In the case of Daniel, as a teenager forcibly inducted into the Nebuchadnezzar School for Public Servants, he sought to be allowed to follow the dietary edicts of the Mosaic law to which he was personally committed, rather than to adopt a Babylonian diet. This might strike us as a rather strange place to draw the line in that there were undoubtedly many other aspects of the school curriculum (such as its teachings about the multiplicity and superiority of the Babylonian gods), which would be even more foreign and unacceptable to a believer in Jehovah.

Nevertheless diet was the issue on which Daniel chose to make a stand personally, and note the way and wisdom with which he went about it. He didn't propose a compromise between the Hebrew and Babylonian diets nor did he go on a hunger strike. Instead he proposed a contest—let me and my three fellow exiles eat and drink what the Mosaic law prescribes, let the other students eat and drink what the Babylonian Food Guide prescribes, and then let's see who is healthier at the end of the day. Most importantly, the point at which he chose to draw the line coincided, not coincidentally, with the movement of God's grace on the heart of his Babylonian custodian who was led to accept rather than reject Daniel's proposal.[17]

With respect to drawing the line on issues of personal morality it is important to allow that not all believers will choose to or be led to draw the line at the same place and we should be careful about "judging another man's servant." Where, for example, if anywhere, does Esther "draw the line"? It can hardly be in accordance with the Jewish laws governing sexual morality—she is an involuntary member of the King Xerxes' harem. Nor is it in the area of diet, the point where Daniel and his companions first drew the line. She eats what they tell her to eat, dresses as they tell her to dress, and conforms in every respect to the rules of the harem and the palace. In the end, however, she draws the line at the one point in common with all the other exiles we have studied—her willingness ultimately to identify with God's people, even if it costs her life.

4. *Identification with the Household of Faith*

Although they were members of a tiny faith-based and ethnically distinctive minority in a hostile environment, the exiles faithfully identified with the household of faith when it was dangerous—even life threatening—to do so. In Joseph's case, he was willing to identify generously and openly with the household of faith to which he truly belonged, even when it was that household which had betrayed him. And he was willing to be publicly identified with the household of faith (his family) despite his awareness that the Egyptians generally loathed nomads, in particular shepherds.[18]

Likewise Daniel, throughout his life, continued to identify with the people of God and the household of faith and to be so identified in the eyes of the Babylonians. With three different rulers whom he served, he is always introduced or referred to as one of the exiles from Judah.[19] Daniel is in Babylon, immersed in the Babylonian culture and administration, but he does not disguise the fact that he is an "exile" and is willing to be known as such.

Cooperation and Compromise

5. *Speaking Unpalatable Truths to Power*

On many occasions these Jewish exiles must have been sorely tempted to compromise the truth in providing advice and counsel to the foreign rulers whom they served—to tell those rulers what they wanted to hear, to flatter them or to sugar-coat the unpalatable, rather than to tell them what they needed to hear. But to their immense credit the exiles "drew the line" at compromising the truth. This is highly relevant since one of the most dangerous things for any leader in any era or system is to be surrounded by people who tell you only what you want to hear.

Joseph told Pharaoh that mighty Egypt was to be brought to her knees by a terrible famine, something Pharaoh undoubtedly didn't want to hear but needed to hear so that grain could be saved and stored away in the bountiful years that were to precede the famine.[20]

Esther had to tell King Xerxes that the man whom he had most trusted and exalted to the highest position in the kingdom, Haman, was an arrogant, vindictive planner of genocide, undeserving of his position or the king's confidence.[21]

Daniel faithfully interpreted "Nebuchadnezzar's Nightmare"—the dream which foretold that Nebuchadnezzar's pride was going to bring him down from his exalted position as the supreme ruler of Babylon to that of an animal grazing on grass and wet by the dew of heaven.[22] And Daniel fearlessly interpreted the handwriting on the wall amid the drunken revelry at Belshazzar's feast—the prediction that the kingdom would be overthrown because of Belshazzar's arrogance and sacrilegious behaviour.[23]

What About Us?

When tempted and challenged to give our supreme allegiance to the systems in which we are embedded—the academy, the school, the company, the market, the charity, the NGO, the church, the team, the party, the department, the government—rather than to God, do we succumb or "draw the line"?

When adverse circumstances and misfortune overwhelm us—the crop fails, our project flops, we fail the test, we lose our job, we lose a loved one, the business goes belly up, the stock market crashes, we lose the election, we lose the war— do we believe that God has abandoned us? Or do we cling to the belief that he is still sovereign over the affairs of humankind and disposes of them as he sees fit?

When tempted and challenged to compromise our personal morals in order to "fit in," do we succumb or "draw the line"?

When we are tempted and challenged to hide or blur our identity as followers of Jesus and children of the Father, do we succumb or "draw the line"?

Cooperation and Compromise

When we are tempted to keep silent in the presence of evil or to substitute half-truth, near-truth, and compromised truth for the whole and unvarnished truth, do we succumb or "draw the line"?

In all these circumstances let us draw insight and inspiration from the lives of the exiles—believers embedded in cultures and systems indifferent or hostile to their faith—who served effectively while remaining faithful to the God who placed and sustained them there.

Notes

1. Genesis 41:41-43
2. Genesis 41:45
3. Daniel 1:1-20
4. "The chief official (Ashpenaz) gave them new names: to Daniel, the name Belteshazzar; to Hananiah, Shadrach; to Mishael, Meshach; and to Azariah, Abednego." Daniel 1:7
5. Daniel 4: 8
6. Daniel 2:48-49; 3:30
7. Modern readers of Vashti's story in the first chapter of the book of Esther might well find themselves admiring her more than Esther. It is Vashti who defies Xerxes' effort to treat and exploit her as a sexual object and who loses her position and influence as a result. Esther, on the other hand, submits to the male-imposed dictates of the harem but in the end uses her beauty and charm to win the favour of the king and save her people.
8. The term "drawing a line in the sand" is frequently used to describe a declaration of principle requiring a decision to adhere to, abandon, or compromise. While I use the term throughout this chapter, it has its limitations as an analogy since "a line drawn in the sand" is subject to alteration or obliteration by any wind that blows and therefore lacks both solidity and permanence as a guide to decision-making or action.
9. Daniel 3:16-18
10. Daniel 3:28
11. Daniel 6:7
12. Daniel 6:10
13. Daniel 6:26
14. Genesis 45:4-9

Notes, *continued*

15. Daniel 4:25
16. Genesis 39:1-20
17. Daniel 1:9
18. Genesis 46:31-34
19. Daniel 2:10; 5:13; 6:13
20. Genesis 41
21. Esther 7
22. Daniel 4
23. Daniel 5

9

Re-establishing the Faith Community Under Hostile Conditions

Spiritual Renewal

Since the days of King David, the spiritual life of Israel and Judah had experienced a long decline, a decline attributed by the prophets to the departure of the people and their rulers from adherence to the law, will, and worship of God. This decline culminated in the Assyrian and Babylonian conquests of the Promised Land and the carrying off of the people of God into slavery and exile in foreign lands. In those foreign lands, under hostile rulers and conditions, the embers of a vital relationship with the living God were kept alive by a faithful few. But would those embers also be extinguished, suffocated by the hostility and unbelief of their environment? Or would they, could they, in the

Re-establishing the Faith Community Under Hostile Conditions

purposes of God be fanned to life again? Was it possible that the spiritual life of the faith community could be revitalized and restored under such conditions?

The same questions are relevant to the Christian community in the 21st century. We too, at least in western Europe and North America, have been in spiritual decline, attributable to the same causes that led to the spiritual decline of Israel and Judah centuries ago. Believers are now a minority in cultures and political systems indifferent or hostile to our faith. And while the embers of a vital relationship with God through Jesus Christ are kept alive by a faithful few, the questions remain: Will they, too, be slowly suffocated by the indifference and hostility of a secular and materialistic environment? Is a genuine renewal of faith in God through Jesus Christ possible under such conditions?

In the case of Judah, a revitalization and restoration of the faith community actually did take place under precisely such conditions. The story of how it came about is told, at least in part, by Ezra and Nehemiah. Both Ezra and Nehemiah were exiles in Babylon and Medo-Persia. Both were used by God to lead the return of a significant portion of the faith community to Jerusalem to rebuild its temple and walls and restore the worship of God. The study of their experience and the lessons derived from it is highly relevant to Christians today who desire a genuine spiritual renewal of the Christian community in our times.

Where Does It Start?

The spiritual renewal described by Ezra and Nehemiah had its beginning in a sovereign and simultaneous movement of God's spirit on two very different kinds of hearts: the hearts of the exiles themselves and, strangely enough, the hearts of their captors—in particular, Cyrus, Darius, and Xerxes, rulers of the Medes and Persians. As we have seen from previous examinations of the lives of exiles such as Joseph, Daniel, and Esther, significant events occur when the sovereign movements of God intersect with human hearts—hearts which either respond to or resist his leading.

In the case of the exiles themselves, Ezra describes those who were led to go and rebuild the house of the Lord in Jerusalem as "everyone whose heart God had moved"—in particular the family heads of Judah and Benjamin, the priests, and the Levites.[1]

This movement of God on the hearts of the faithful few appeared to manifest itself in two ways as reflected in the prayers of exiles like Daniel[2] and, later, Nehemiah.[3] It moved them to:

- Acknowledge and repent of the acts and attitudes that had led to their people's alienation from the person, will, and work of God in the first place.

- Reaffirm and reassert their faith in the promises of God, in particular the promise communicated by Jeremiah that in due time God would restore his relationship with the faithful and restore them to their place of worship in Jerusalem.

In the case of the rulers of the Medes and the Persians during whose reign this restoration took place, Ezra asserts that "the Lord moved the heart of Cyrus king of Persia" to make the proclamation that authorized it.[4] When the enemies of the Jews who had inhabited Judah during the exile endeavoured to stop the work by advising the king that Jerusalem had a history of rebellion, letters were sent from Ezra to the Persian rulers defending their right to proceed.[5] In the end, both Darius the Mede and Xerxes re-authorized the rebuilding of the temple and the city, starting with its walls, leading Ezra to exclaim, "Praise be to the Lord, the God of our fathers, who has put it into the king's heart to bring honour to the house of the Lord in Jerusalem in this way and who has extended his good favour to me before the king and his advisers and all the king's powerful officials."[6]

It is significant that both Ezra and Nehemiah give as much attention to recording the "movement of God" on the hearts of the Median and Persian rulers as they do to the movement of God on the hearts of his own people.

The Response of the Faithful to the Movement of God in Their Hearts

The great prayer of the exile Daniel, recorded in the ninth chapter of the book of Daniel, provides a classic and instructive model of the prayer for spiritual renewal:

> In the first year of Darius son of Xerxes (a Mede by descent), who was made ruler over the Babylonian kingdom—in the first year of his reign, I, Daniel, understood from the Scriptures, according to the word of the LORD given to Jeremiah the prophet, that the desolation of Jerusalem would last seventy years. So I turned to the Lord God and pleaded with him in prayer and petition, in fasting, and in sackcloth and ashes.
>
> I prayed to the LORD my God and confessed:
>
> "Lord, the great and awesome God, who keeps his covenant of love with those who love him and keep his commandments, we have sinned and done wrong. We have been wicked and have rebelled; we have turned away from your commands and laws. We have not listened to your servants the prophets, who spoke in your name to our kings, our princes and our ancestors, and to all the people of the land.
>
> "Lord, you are righteous, but this day we are covered with shame—the people of Judah and the inhabitants of Jerusalem and all Israel, both near and far, in all the countries where you have scattered us because of our

Re-establishing the Faith Community Under Hostile Conditions

unfaithfulness to you. We and our kings, our princes and our ancestors are covered with shame, Lord, because we have sinned against you. The Lord our God is merciful and forgiving, even though we have rebelled against him; we have not obeyed the Lord our God or kept the laws he gave us through his servants the prophets. All Israel has transgressed your law and turned away, refusing to obey you. ...

"Now, Lord our God, who brought your people out of Egypt with a mighty hand and who made for yourself a name that endures to this day, we have sinned, we have done wrong. Lord, in keeping with all your righteous acts, turn away your anger and your wrath from Jerusalem, your city, your holy hill. Our sins and the iniquities of our ancestors have made Jerusalem and your people an object of scorn to all those around us.

"Now, our God, hear the prayers and petitions of your servant. For your sake, Lord, look with favor on your desolate sanctuary. Give ear, our God, and hear; open your eyes and see the desolation of the city that bears your Name. We do not make requests of you because we are righteous, but because of your great mercy. Lord, listen! Lord, forgive! Lord, hear and act! For your sake, my God, do not delay, because your city and your people bear your Name."[7]

There is of course much to be learned concerning the conditions and factors which have led to the periodic renewal of the Christian faith down through the centuries from the vast library of scholarly work that exists on this subject. I refer particularly to works on the history and nature of such "movements of God" as the Reformation, the Counter-Reformation, the First and Second Great Awakenings, and national and local "revivals." The latter would include those that have occurred in Wales, Scotland, and New England, and more recently in Africa, Latin America, and Asia.

This is not the place to more thoroughly analyze and discuss those factors and conditions and their relevance to our day and age, nor am I suitably qualified to do so. I would, however, encourage each of us to begin to identify from our own perspective what a genuine, divinely inspired renewal of the Christian faith in our time might look like, particularly within Canada.

From my own perspective as a Christian in politics, by referring to the need for a renewal of the Christian faith in our time I am not referring to some restoration of the past political influence of Christianity. I am not referring to the "gaining of control" by professing Christians over the institutions and services of the state, nor am I referring to some dramatic increase in the size and impressiveness of church attendance, church buildings, or church budgets.

Rather I believe that such a spiritual renewal should manifest itself in the following ways:

- In a renewal of our awareness of evil and its roots in our own lives and in the world in which we live, including the diabolical nature of the violence, crime, addictions, injustices, and self-destructive obsessions that afflict so many human lives today.[8]

- In a renewed passion for healthy relationships with ourselves, our families, our neighbours, our environment, and our Creator.

- In a renewed concern leading to action on behalf of the poor, the sick, and the victims of injustice and oppression.

- In a renewed faith in the reality of God and the love of God for humankind, and his willingness and ability to communicate with us and transform us from within.

- In a renewed belief in the efficacy of spiritual practices such as prayer and Scripture study which draw us closer to him, and the necessity and benefits of spiritual fellowship.

- And most importantly, in a renewed vision of who Jesus Christ is and what he has to offer in terms of deliverance from evil, the healing of broken relationships, and enabling self-sacrificial service on behalf of others.

The Response of Political Leaders to the Movement of God on Their Hearts

For a person with political interests and involvements, the most striking aspect of the restoration of the exiled faith community as described in the books of Ezra and Nehemiah is the role of rulers who did not share that faith in facilitating its restoration.

The prayer of Daniel previously cited indicates what the movement of God on the hearts of the exiles moved *them* to do—to pray, to repent, and to claim his promises for renewal. Likewise Ezra's citing of the proclamation of King Cyrus of Persia in the first year of his reign indicates what the movement of God on the heart of this political ruler moved *him* to proclaim throughout his realm:

> "This is what Cyrus king of Persia says: 'The LORD, the God of heaven, has given me all the kingdoms of the earth and he has appointed me to build a temple for him at Jerusalem in Judah. Any of his people among you may go up to Jerusalem in Judah and build the temple of the LORD, the God of Israel, the God who is in Jerusalem, and may their God be with them. And in any locality where survivors may now be living, the people are to provide them with silver and gold, with goods and livestock, and with freewill offerings for the temple of God in Jerusalem.' "[9]

Here then is a pertinent question for those longing and praying for a renewal of the Christian faith in our time. Should we also be looking for some movement of God on the heart of some secular political leader who does not share that faith but which would nevertheless facilitate genuine spiritual renewal and complement the movement of God on

Re-establishing the Faith Community Under Hostile Conditions

the hearts of his own people?

In a secular, pluralist state such as Canada, this facilitating and complementary action by a political leader or government could not take the form of an explicit endorsement or provision of support for the Christian faith and its institutional forms. But it could conceivably take the form of a genuine and renewed championing of freedom of conscience and belief from which not only Christians but also others with faith-based convictions would benefit.

The historians tell us that Cyrus the Great of Persia was a remarkable ruler for that age and time in that he did not try to impose the religion of Persia on the nations and peoples he conquered. Rather, he was magnanimous in allowing captive peoples to retain and even restore their traditional religious practices.[10]

In a similar vein, one of the first major acts of the Roman Emperor Constantine (Emperor from 306 to 337 AD and the first Emperor to claim conversion to Christianity) involved proclamation of the Edict of Milan in 313 AD. Contrary to popular opinion, the Edict did not make Christianity the official religion of the Empire (this came much later in 380 AD). Instead, it expressly granted religious liberty not only to Christians who had been the targets of ruthless persecution but also to the practitioners of all religions throughout the Empire.[11]

It was the granting of such freedom of conscience and

practice, as much as the favour of the Emperor himself, that then permitted the Christian faith to flourish and expand its influence throughout the Empire.

If there was one thing a secular political leader, for example, in Canada, could do to facilitate a renewal of the Christian faith in our time without explicitly endorsing or supporting it, it would be simply to ensure that the guarantees of freedom of conscience and belief contained in our Charter of Rights and Freedoms are actually honoured and accorded in practice to those whose consciences and beliefs are rooted in a faith perspective, just as those guarantees are presently applied aggressively to expressions of conscience and belief rooted in secular and non-religious (even anti-religious) perspectives.[12] Such a genuine renewal of freedom of conscience and belief in Canada, in particular freedom from the dictates of political correctness and the imposition of secular values by our media, academic, judicial, and political elites on those who do not share those perspectives, might be highly conducive to a renewal of genuine Christian faith in our time.

The Need for Caution

In scanning the political horizon for proclamations or actions by secular leaders and governments which might, even inadvertently or indirectly, facilitate a renewal and reinvigoration of faith in Christ, it is especially important to guard against the dangers of such leaders using a revival of religion for strictly political reasons.

In Russia, for example, while it is dangerous to impute motives to leaders most of us only know about through the media, Vladimir Putin's efforts to revitalize the role and influence of the Eastern Orthodox church would appear to be more related to his interest in stimulating a revival of Russian nationalism than it is to restoring the influence of the Christian faith in Russian society.

In the same vein, I recall a conversation I had a number of years ago with a Chinese Communist official concerning the professed efforts of his party to stamp out corruption. He acknowledged that "religion" in many societies had played a role in establishing and enforcing moral standards such as "Thou shalt not steal." While it would be inconceivable for the Communist Party of China, being atheistic in principle, to consider facilitating a renewal of theistic religions for the purposes of combatting corruption, it was not inconceivable that it could facilitate renewed interest in a non-theistic religion such as Confucianism and harness it to that task.[13]

Can Christian Believers Learn from Secular Efforts to Restore the Morale of Demoralized Organizations?

One of the strangest and most arresting stories told by Jesus of Nazareth was about an "unjust steward." The man was about to be sacked from his position by his master so he used his last days on the job to ensure a favourable position for himself with his master's debtors by writing down their debt notes. While Jesus was obviously not condoning the dishonesty of the unjust steward, he did draw attention to his "shrewdness" and what might be learned from it, remarking that "the people of this world are more shrewd in dealing with their own kind than are the people of the light."[14]

Without carrying this line of reasoning too far, it might nevertheless be helpful to those longing for a renewal of the faith community—weakened and demoralized by past defeats and years in exile in hostile environments—also to study some of the examples of successful attempts to restore the vigour and morale of non-religious communities and organizations that have been "down and out."

This is a subject that political leaders must frequently consider, especially after one personally loses an election or one's political party has suffered a devastating and demoralizing electoral defeat. In my case, a "rebuilding story" which I have found most instructive is that involving the revitalization of the British Army in Burma during the Second World War as told by its leader, Field-Marshall Viscount William Slim.[15]

In 1942 the British Army was systematically driven back across Burma by the Japanese all the way to India, suffering defeat after defeat and horrendous casualties along the way.

Re-establishing the Faith Community Under Hostile Conditions

After retreating to India, its shaken leader, William Slim, was instructed to rebuild its ranks, rebuild its morale, and rebuild its fighting capacity—all of which he did. This reinvigorated army then successfully fought all the way back across Burma and by 1945 secured complete victory over the retreating Japanese forces.

Slim's memoir, *Defeat into Victory,* is regarded as a military classic and is still studied at military academies around the world. In it he urges the leaders of defeated and demoralized troops to "remember only the lessons to be learned from defeat—they are more than from victory."

He then specifically addresses the question of how to restore the morale of a defeated army, defining morale as a "state of mind ... which will move a whole group of men to give their last ounce to achieve something, without counting the cost to themselves." He goes on to say that if that morale is to endure, "... it must have certain foundations ... spiritual, intellectual, and material, and that is the order of their importance."[16]

Slim uses the word "spiritual" not in its strictly religious meaning but as "belief in a cause," in particular, a just cause, a "great and noble object" larger than one's self and self-preservation. Slim would likely argue that an army whose members' sole interest is in "saving themselves" will never experience victory in the broader sense, something that we evangelicals with our heavy emphasis on personal salvation need to reflect upon. His observations and perspectives are well worth study by anyone involved in efforts to renew the morale and effectiveness of a defeated and demoralized community, including a faith community.

Summary of Lessons from the Lives of the Exiles

As we close these lessons in leadership from the lives of believers living in exile it is appropriate for each of us to ask what aspects of their experience are most meaningful and applicable to us personally.

Is it their faith in the sovereignty of God—the belief encouraged by the inspired words of Jeremiah instructing them to settle down, to build, to pray, to disregard false spiritual advice, and to trust in the providence and promises of God—even in dire circumstances and while living in societies and organizations hostile to their faith?

Is it the realization that God can and does use major disasters and calamities in the lives of individuals and nations to lead and place believers in positions of influence and authority that they might not otherwise come to occupy—economic crises, environmental crises, health crises—at the international, national, local, and personal levels? Could it be that he is even now using some such crisis in your life or community to position you for service in advancing his kingdom and the wellbeing of others?

Re-establishing the Faith Community Under Hostile Conditions

Have we perhaps gained from these studies a deeper understanding of the perverse spiritual dialectic whereby the author of evil endeavours to twist things that are in themselves good or potentially good—faith, science, freedom, public and private service bureaucracies—toward evil and destructive ends? Has that understanding strengthened our resolve to guard against and resist such abuses? And have we gained insights into opportunities and means for doing so—such as protesting and addressing the abuse of freedom by extremists, including religious extremists, or recognizing and addressing the dark side of science, technology, and bureaucratic organizations?

Have we also gained from these studies a deeper appreciation of the grace and work of God in preventing such transformations of good into evil and in effecting counter-transformations of evil or potential evil into good? Have we resolved to enter into God's work of counter-transformation in some way?

With respect to safeguarding and "delivering from evil" the bureaucratic organizations in which so many of us as believers find ourselves embedded today, do we sense ourselves being led:

- To insist that other care-giving alternatives be considered before automatically consigning persons in need to such systems?

Leadership Lessons from the Lives of the Exiles

- To frequently visit the "front lines" of such organizations and expose ourselves to the conditions and experience of those who work there and those whom they serve?

- To be, within such organizations, that ethical salt and light of which Jesus spoke—to listen to that still, small voice of our spiritually sensitized consciences and to follow its dictates?

- To accept responsibility for some of the negative outcomes of bureaucratic organizations and behaviours, even at personal cost?

Have we, through examining the lives of the exiles, gained a deeper appreciation of where and how to "draw the line" between cooperation with those systems and cultures in which we are embedded and actions which compromise our faith? Have we ourselves "drawn the line" at some point in our own circumstances—for example, at the point of:

- Granting our ultimate allegiance to God and not to someone or something else?

- Upholding rather than compromising some personal moral standard?

- Identifying with rather than disassociating ourselves from the faith community?

- Being willing rather than reluctant to speak uncompromised truth to power?

Re-establishing the Faith Community Under Hostile Conditions

Finally, have we been challenged to pray for and participate in some way in the restoration of faith in Christ in our times and circumstances through the movement of God on our own hearts and on the hearts of those responsible for our public affairs?

All of the above are valuable "lessons in leadership from the lives of the exiles"—believers in another time and space embedded in cultures and organizations indifferent or hostile to their faith. May those of us who find ourselves providentially embedded in similar situations today derive inspiration and guidance from their experience.

Notes

1. Ezra 1:5
2. Daniel 9:1-19
3. Nehemiah 1:4-11
4. Ezra 1:1-4
5. Ezra 4:6-6:12
6. Ezra 7:27-28
7. Daniel 9:1-19
8. Since we invariably reap what we sow, is not any society which increasingly entertains itself by viewing, hearing, and reading about evil, increasingly likely to be afflicted in real life by those very same evils? Do we not need a heightened awareness of the possibility that for every murder, assault, and deception whereby we entertain ourselves via our literature, movies, plays, and video screens, we may well be destined to experience real-life murders, assaults, and deceptions on our streets and in our communities? Although the context is different, the principle is the same as that referred to by Abraham Lincoln in his second inaugural address when he declared: "Fondly do we hope, fervently do we pray, that this mighty scourge of war may speedily pass away. Yet, if God wills that it continue until all the wealth piled by the bondsman's two hundred and fifty years of unrequited toil shall be sunk, and until every drop of blood drawn with the lash shall be paid by another drawn with the sword, as was said three thousand years ago, so still it must be said 'the judgments of the Lord are true and righteous altogether.' " Second Inaugural Address, Abraham Lincoln (March 4, 1865).
9. Ezra 1:2-4
10. A famous document inscribed in clay and dated to the days just after Cyrus's conquest of Babylon describes how Cyrus

Notes, *continued*

had improved the lives of the citizens of Babylonia, repatriated displaced peoples, and restored temples and cult sanctuaries. This "Cyrus Cylinder" is preserved at the British Museum in London; while some scholars dispute its interpretation, it is generally accepted that Cyrus permitted considerable religious liberty among those peoples and nations he conquered.

11. "When you see that this has been granted to [Christians] by us, your Worship will know that we have also conceded to other religions the right of open and free observance of their worship for the sake of the peace of our times, that each one may have the free opportunity to worship as he pleases; this regulation is made that we may not seem to detract from any dignity of any religion." Quoted from "Edict of Milan," Lactantius, On the Deaths of the Persecutors (*De mortibus persecutorum*), ch. 48. opera, ed. 0. F. Fritzsche, II, p 288 sq. (Bibl Patr. Ecc. Lat.).

12. Part I, Canadian Charter of Rights and Freedoms, Clause 2, reads: "Everyone has the following fundamental Freedoms: (a) freedom of conscience and religion; (b) freedom of thought, belief, opinion and expression, including freedom of the press and other media communication; (c) freedom of peaceful assembly; and (d) freedom of association." (The Constitution Act, 1982, Schedule B to the Canada Act 1982 (UK), 1982, c 11.).

13. The Chinese government has been encouraging the revival of Confucianism, including the teaching of Confucian classics in secondary schools and promoting Confucianism abroad through the Confucius Institute. An editorial from the Herald Tribune entitled "China's leaders rediscover Confucianism" can be found at http://www.nytimes.com/2006/09/14/opinion/14iht-edbell.2807200.html?_r=0 (accessed August 19, 2015).

Notes, *continued*

14. Luke 16:8

15. Field-Marshal Viscount William Slim, *Defeat into Victory: Battling Japan in Burma and India, 1942-1945* (Cooper Square Press, 2000).

16. Ibid., p.182

Preston Manning served as a member of the Canadian House of Commons from 1993 to 2001. He founded two new political parties—the Reform Party of Canada and the Canadian Reform Conservative Alliance—and was the Leader of the Official Opposition from 1997 to 2000. In 2005, he founded the Manning Centre for Building Democracy, which supports research, educational, and communications initiatives designed to achieve a more democratic society in Canada guided by conservative principles. He was appointed a Companion of the Order of Canada in 2007 and has received honorary doctorates from five Canadian universities. Preston Manning became a Senior Fellow of the Marketplace Institute in January 2012.